# Action-Oriented Approaches to Regional Development Planning

edited by
# Avrom Bendavid-Val
# Peter P. Waller

# Action-Oriented Approaches to Regional Development Planning

PRAEGER SPECIAL STUDIES IN INTERNATIONAL ECONOMICS AND DEVELOPMENT

**Praeger Publishers**   New York   Washington   London

Library of Congress Cataloging in Publication Data
Main entry under title:

Action-oriented approaches to regional development planning.

    (Praeger special studies in international economics and
development)
    Bibliography: p.
    Includes index.
    1. Regional planning.   2. Economic development.
I. Bendavid-Val, Avrom.  II.  Waller, Peter P.
HT391.A25     309.2'5     75-3746
ISBN 0-275-07430-7

PRAEGER PUBLISHERS
111 Fourth Avenue, New York, N.Y. 10003, U.S.A.

Published in the United States of America in 1975
by Praeger Publishers, Inc.

Printed in the United States of America

This book may strike the reader as a strange (but, hopefully, useful) collection of papers. It is a heterogeneous collection. Some chapters are more philosophical than others; some are regionally oriented; some, methodologically oriented; some, downright technical. All but the first are authored by members of the German Development Institute. They reflect differences in temperament, style, and ideology that prevail among the contributing authors. They reflect three years of collaboration between the editors, during which some of the case studies described were under way. There is but a single principal theme that motivated the collaboration on this book and that unifies its chapters: the desire to develop and promote action-oriented approaches to regional development planning, in an effort to improve on its past dismal performance in leading to meaningful development.

So the reader is cautioned: This book is not intended to provide guidelines for <u>development</u>; its subject, rather, concerns approaches to <u>planning</u> as a process employed in the interest of development. Thus, within most chapters there will be found a description of a case-study region and a proposed development program of some sort. The purpose of the presentation, however, is in all cases to show the reader the process used to get from one to the other quickly and in a way that produces a development program with a high probability of having prompt positive impacts. It was not the particular development "solutions" that provided the basis for inclusion of the articles.

This book is designed for people who are busy and busily involved in regional development in developing countries at an operational level. Its purpose, like that of action-oriented planning itself, is to provide them with alternative tools of the sort not usually described in the literature, quickly, clearly, and in a form ready for application. Yet, since planning is a creative activity, this cannot be a handbook. It should be viewed as a compendium of ideas that can stimulate creativity in responding to the unique needs of each unique region and each unique planning situation.

Part I contains two essays on a purely philosophical-methodological level. They are very dissimilar, but, on reflection, they will be found to be much more similar than they first appeared. Both offer suggestions for dealing with the fact that "comprehensive" planning does not work and that a straight "project" approach is, on historical evidence, imprudent. They have in common a more realistic apprehension of the usefulness of quantification and formal models than more traditional approaches. They both aim at a reduction of the time-consuming process of data collection, and they truly try to direct it toward those data that are really needed for the decisions to be made.

Action-oriented planning must not only be quick, however; it must also produce implementable projects and be easily understood by those who have to implement the measures it recommends. Thus, both approaches are organized about a logical sequence of planning steps that can be controlled by the decision makers and the implementing administration. Neither approach includes the use of models of optimum allocation among alternative projects, because both recognize that in reality the problem is more to identify viable projects than to choose among them. Ultimately, however, the search for concrete projects, to which both approaches are directed, has to be guided by some overriding goals or overall strategy. The way in which this is accomplished is the essential feature characterizing the action-oriented approach. And it is here that the two approaches differ.

Part II deals with case-study applications. These are reports of varying field experiences, with attempts to apply the approach outlined in Chapter 2, or some part or modified form of it. The Madagascar case follows rather strictly the sequence of planning steps as suggested by the reduced-planning approach. Certain points, such as identification of felt needs, however, are not covered in detail. Both the Kosi and the Gwembe cases give more insight. The Madagascar case is also more of the general type, with a whole list of projects in various sectors. The search process in the Kosi region, on the other hand, led to the identification of one key project that was to solve the bottleneck of the development of the study region. In the Wollega case, for lack of development potential in other sectors, analysis was concentrated in one sector: agriculture. This case also demonstrates the necessity of detailed planning of the implementation phase.

In Part III specific methods, rather than planning approaches, are discussed. But, again, the methods represent an attempt to provide an action-oriented input to the regional-development-planning process. Out of the many methods available two are demonstrated as examples: a social information system in health planning (Gwembe case) and the elaboration of an input-output table (Arequipa case).

Obviously, those recorded here are not the only possible action-oriented approaches. But a literature on the subject is lacking, so the interested reader cannot merely go to his library to cover the field. He will have to remain alert to the occasional article, suggestion, or creative idea that comes along through one means or another and that can provide insight into additional action-oriented approaches. These can always be tested, as should the ideas in this book, with the criteria suggested by Dr. Waller in Chapter 2. One should ask whether they provide a key to action-orientation, reduction in analytical work, integration of program elements, flexibility of planning, and participation of the population.

# CONTENTS

# PART III: METHODS

## LIST OF TABLES, CHARTS, AND MAPS

# 1

# THE THEMES-STRATEGY-PROJECTS APPROACH TO PLANNING FOR REGIONAL DEVELOPMENT

Avrom Bendavid-Val

## THE NEED FOR A MIDDLE GROUND

At a recent development symposium a learned professor with many years experience in development rose to the podium to declare:

> I believe that projects are the only thing that matters. Nothing has come of all the planning I have done, but the projects remain. Even if we cannot quantify their anticipated benefits, or guarantee there will be any, we must spend our time and money putting up projects, not drawing up plans. When planners leave, nothing remains. When the builders leave, a monument stays behind, testifying that man is changing the landscape; and the people see and feel that development is taking place.

Most serious development analysts and planners reject the idea of a pure "projects" approach, where the primary concern is with putting up projects, usually with a bias toward those that are highly visible, and in any case not within any coordinated development framework. Yet if this approach has little to recommend it, the alternatives have not proven themselves either.

---

This chapter is based on two articles that appeared in the International Development Review (1972/1 and 1973/3). I am grateful for the enlightened policy of the Society for International Development regarding the rights of authors to make subsequent use of articles published in the IDR.

Short-term planning (one year or so) is not really planning but more on the order of "action programming." It does not come in place of other planning but is supposed to put short-term teeth into the longer-term plans. Long-term planning (20 or more years) is not really taken seriously by anyone anyway. Despite the admirable mathematical perfection that long-term-planning models often boast, there is not a long-term planner in the business who would risk investing his own money on the basis of such a plan. Most reasonable men agree that the function of a long-term plan is to provide perspective for the shorter term and that long-term plans, if they are to serve even this function, should be revised well before a fraction of the period they cover has passed.

That leaves intermediate-term planning (five to ten years), which in fact is what is meant by the term "development planning," as conventionally used with regard to developing countries and regions. Such planning usually involves an intricate system of targets and behavioral models and in effect says, "Given certain assumptions, and having established certain parameters, we must affect certain variables in specified degrees and directions in order to achieve specified goals." Ideally, the plan would go on to say how that can be done. While the logic of this kind of planning seems irrefutable on the face of it, most of us have been sorely disillusioned by its performance over the last decade or two.

We know that the reasons for the poor performance of conventional development planning are to be found in the unavailability--and perhaps even more in the unreliability--of the data inputs upon which it relies; in the long list of unpredictables for which such planning cannot account; in the instability of the political environment; in the tendency for plans to be static and lifeless (that is, once completed, such plans tend to be unresponsive even to the very dynamics they may have set in motion), and in much more. We know that these features of the development setting tend to be even more widespread and more severe at the subnational, regional level, where, among other things, lack of accuracy has less opportunity than at the national level to get swallowed up in overwhelming aggregates. And we know that they tend to reduce the conventional, often mathematically sophisticated techniques of planning to largely academic exercises, bearing little relationship to the realities of the present, and probably no relevance for the realities of the future.

We need to focus on a meaningful middle ground for regional development planning between the unacceptable primitiveness of an isolated projects approach and the widely demonstrated futility of the conventional planning approach.

## THE UN/IPD TEAM FOR NORTHERN THAILAND

When the UN/IPD Team for the Development of the Northern
Region of Thailand first set to work in mid-1970, its work program
called for an approach more or less of the conventional variety.  It
did not take many weeks of field work for the planners to conclude,
however, that the region represented a classical case of a development setting inappropriate to planning in a conventional sense.  The
team was fully capable of designing a plan using all the latest optimization and other techniques, and in fact several exercises toward
that end were undertaken.  But it became clear that such a plan would
ultimately contribute more to filling up empty spaces on government
bookshelves than to meaningful development of the region.  And so
the team turned to what appeared to be the only alternate approach.

Work on models and systems tapered off, and a flurry of activity aimed at identifying useful projects ensued.  Planning was now
to be "project oriented."  Unlike some projects of an earlier generation, however, projects were now to be well thought out and demon-
strably "bankable" in accordance with World Bank criteria.  As the
team crossed the halfway mark in the designated life-span of the
planning effort, quite a few very sensible and original ideas for
projects had been formulated and were winning approval from various officials.  The planning team seemed to have hit upon an approach that was pragmatic, realistic, simple, and well-suited to
the particular development setting.

But the team had not had the opportunity to stand aside and
clearly view the evolution in its thinking.  Its members had operated
by feel and intuition rather than in accordance with a formulated
"project approach," and while the basis for any particular action or
decision could be explained, the overall conceptual underpinnings
for what they had been doing were never formalized and, therefore,
were nowhere articulated.  When the conclusion of the initial planning effort loomed just over the horizon six to nine months hence,
thought turned to the way in which the fruit of the team's work
would be integrated into a written plan.  Would the "plan" simply be
a sector-by-sector exposition of the recommended projects, ac-
companied by the usual sort of data compendium?  Could it be
claimed that that was planning?  Did that really represent the sum
of the planning team's accomplishments?  The time had clearly arrived for a self-examination, for the formulation of the implicit
central concept that had been guiding the planning activity, for the
determination of what remained to be done in conformity with that
concept, and for a reassessment of the team's recommendations in
light of that concept.

In a series of team meetings events of the past months of work were reviewed, and from the self-examination two major points emerged. First, the concept of overall planning had not actually been abandoned, though a conventional approach to planning had. It turned out that some of the information gathered during the early efforts toward a conventional-style plan had served as a partial basis for understanding the major economic strengths and weaknesses of the region. This understanding had, in turn, to some extent guided research with respect to each of the sectors and branches in the region. Moreover, each of the specialists on the team had, as a result of his investigations, evolved a general "development strategy" for his area of concern that had guided him in project identification. Those "sectoral" strategies had remained largely unwritten and unformalized, but through casual conversation the team members had been influencing each other's thoughts and thus inadvertently sowing the seeds for the formulation of an integrated overall strategy for development of the region. Second, the concept of a "project" had, by unspoken agreement, been allowed to evolve from "bankability" to one that encompassed virtually any development-oriented action. Though the fact had not been formalized or even articulated, the team had been groping toward that middle ground between conventional planning and isolated projects.

The larger approach with which the unarticulated judgments of the team members appeared consistent was identified, formulated, and expanded in subsequent team meetings into a full-fledged planning approach. The overriding simplicity of the approach enabled the planners, even at that late date, to go back to the starting point, consider how their approaches had so far fit together, fill in the gaps, integrate their findings and conclusions as the logic of the approach dictated, and proceed with the identification of additional projects.

The approach formulated is presented below in its broadest terms and is followed by a section providing some further elaboration and clarification.


## THE THEMES-STRATEGY-PROJECTS APPROACH

The themes-strategy-projects (TSP) approach to planning for regional development directs the analysis and planning process through a logical three-step sequence, from the general to the specific.

## Step 1:  Determination of Key Strategy Themes

The key strategy themes are determinated on the basis of a general regional analysis employing the most readily available data. Such data are usually generated by central rather than by regional or other local agencies, and if not entirely accurate, they tend at least to be consistent with respect to any single source.  Consequently, they are adequate for preliminary trend detection and a variety of interareal and intertemporal comparative analyses.  For example, through examination of regional time-series data, comparison with national data and data on other regions, and a certain amount of ingenuity coupled with a personal familiarity with the region, analysis might be made of regional output by branch, productivity, public investment, employment, and more, depending upon data availability. All of this could be considered on a per capita basis as well, and a variety of social variables might also be considered.  Since this analysis deals with broad aggregates, it tends to view the region as a single entity, within the national and interregional contexts.

The first general regional analysis should be relatively easy to perform and not especially time-consuming.  It is important not to get bogged down in detail or excessive concern with data accuracy in this step of the sequence.  Performing the analysis has important obvious side-benefits for the planning team in terms of familiarization with the region and the nature of available data, crystallization of working relationships, establishment of first contacts with various agencies, and so on.

The key themes determined on the basis of such an analysis might be viewed as "macrothemes."  This might include, for example, the need for a more favorable industry mix (with the desired direction of change in specific sectors and branches spelled out), the need for diversification, the need for an increase in the income multiplier, the need for increased productivity, the need for a larger share of the national public investment budget, the need for rationalization in certain industries, the need for improved housing, and the like.  These are the broad "oughts"; guiding themes that may feature overlap, may rest on minimal quantitative analysis, and may smack of the ideal, since the precise "what" and "how" of each theme are not addressed.

The key strategy themes together constitute the overall thematic structure within which growth must take place and toward which it should be oriented, if it is to bring about meaningful long-term development.  Moreover, the framework of key strategy themes is instrumental in establishing planning priorities (not to be confused

with development priorities) and, therefore, in providing guidance
for allocating the usually severely limited research and planning resources available for more detailed work.

But that should not be taken to mean that once determined, the
key strategy themes may not be changed during the planning process.
The themes framework does not include all the relevant strategy
themes possible for the region in question—only the key ones.  Subsequent detailed research may show that what was earlier thought to
be key is in fact not so, and the other way around.  The key themes
can be changed and refined as their context is better understood,
even after work has progressed to the next level of specificity.  But
they nevertheless should remain the guiding framework at the broadest level of generalization.


### Step 2:  Determination of Overall Strategy
### for Development

The overall strategy for the development of the region is based
on detailed investigations of the various components of the regional
complex.  These investigations obtain at least their themes.  While
the investigations may be performed by individual specialists, it is
essential that a high degree of coordination prevail and that findings
be constantly exchanged.  In this way there is always a sense of the
whole, and the overall strategy that is ultimately derived from the
investigations can be woven of their interrelated conclusions.

The overall strategy for development is a program that spells
out the approach to be taken with respect to each of the various aspects of the region's economic, social, and administrative activity.
As such, it provides the specific framework for project recommendations.  Since it is based upon detailed investigations, the overall
strategy relates to the real problems and potentials in each area of
regional activity and reflects the behavioral links between those activities and the key strategy themes.  It considers the interregional
and intraregional spatial framework; the economic branches per se,
as well as the supporting systems; the national setting and national
goals; the time element as a strategy factor; and sociocultural elements of the regional fabric.  The overall strategy for development
of the region is realistic because it rests on a deeper knowledge of
the region's available and potential human, institutional, natural,
and capital resources.  It is specific but stops short of actual project
recommendations.

## Step 3: Project Recommendations

The project recommendations are based on yet more detailed but narrow-range investigations. Guidance for these will derive primarily from research carried out in step 2. Suggestions may, of course, come from other sources as well. The studies carried out in connection with project recommendations are not only more detailed but also of a completely different nature from those performed under step 2. What these studies should encompass will be clear from the following elaboration of the concepts "project" and "project recommendation."

A project that may be recommended is, for purposes of this planning approach, any action that will bring about a change in the nature or quantity of production in the region, in the supporting systems (including administration), in social welfare, or in the spatial framework. It is a rather broad concept. Establishing a new factory, an experimental crop, a dam, a regional development commission, a regional college, village health centers, low-income tourist facilities, an extension-services network, or a regional small-scale technology center would all be "projects."

"Project recommendations" are set forth within the framework of the overall strategy for development of the region, and it should thus be clear how each fits in and ultimately responds to the key strategy themes. A project recommendation includes the identification of the project; a demonstration (preliminary and rough) of its apparent feasibility, including preliminary cost estimates and source of funding; a broad assessment of likely impacts, both short-run and long-run; an indication of intersectoral implications; a program of actions or procedures that must be undertaken to get the project under way; and the machinery that must be set up for a continuous review of the project and to ensure its proper implementation. The project recommendations stop short of full-fledged feasibility studies or detailed physical or other plans for any project.

## After the TSP Sequence

The TSP sequence would, of course, be followed, first, by detailed studies and plans of the type usually associated more with the implementation of specific projects than with regional planning and, then, by direct implementation activities. Yet the sequence of logical steps does not even end there, for implementation and planning must ultimately become integrated components of a single ongoing

process.  Thus, the TSP approach should be thought of as a continuing activity, with the sequence of planning steps run through and revised, say, on an annual or biannual basis.  In this way, changes in
the larger setting and the impacts of implemented projects are incorporated into the analysis and may bring about a revision of key
themes and overall strategy.  These thereby become a dynamic
framework for project review and for the generation of new project
recommendations.

## MORE ON THE TSP APPROACH

What follows is perhaps central to understanding the applicability of the TSP approach, particularly in the developing countries, for
the approach has been formulated with the features of the development setting commonly found in the developing countries chiefly in
mind.

### Themes Versus Goals

It will be noted that at no point in the TSP cycle are "regional
goals and objectives" specifically declared, as such.  It is believed
that such declarations usually advance the art of polemics more than
the development of regions.  Apart from universally recognized development goals, such as "improved standard of living," the goals
and objectives of the development program are implicit, if not explicit, in the key strategy themes and the overall strategy for development.
It might appear that if targets have not been specified, there
is no relevant standard against which to measure progress.  But the
fact is we are almost never satisfied with the progress we make toward predetermined targets:  If targets have been achieved or sur-
passed, we tend to conclude that they were too modest; if they are
not achieved, we tend to conclude that they were too ambitious.  In
no case will the fact that we nave specified quantified targets influence the degree to which we strain to achieve progress as measured
by the chosen indicators.  More will be said on the subject of evaluation later.
It can be (and has been) argued that since the key strategy
themes provide the framework for strategy determination, they cannot possibly differ in substance from the traditional concepts of
goals, targets, or objectives--terms with which planners are more
comfortable.  But goals, targets, objectives, and the like are parts
of planning systems woven of a number of such components, all

tightly interdependent.  An element is included in such a system only
when its behavioral relationships with the other elements can, at
least in theory or by assumption, be precisely specified and pre-
dicted.  Thus, conventionally, goals and targets are quantified, and
they are declared only after extensive analytical work of the mathematical variety.

Not so with the key strategy themes.  They derive from a preliminary empirical analysis based on readily available data, combined with other analyses based on first- and second-hand familiarity with the region.  They are not part of a system but rather the
outcome of the first step in an approach, which means that they are
part of a learning process.  Therefore, they do not require the kind
of justification and theoretical confirmation that mathematical models
of the highly sophisticated genre provide.

Where a goal or target might be expressed, "Raise regional
investment to an annual level of x percent in Q years," a key strategy
theme might be, "Obtain a more equitable share of the national investment budget and raise the level of private investment substan-
tially." While targets provide the development plan with a precise
direction and destination, key strategy themes are a means of rapid-
ly providing the basis and direction for more detailed work concerning specific components (sectors, branches) of the regional complex, toward strategy determination.  The key strategy themes are
themes, not goals, for the planning and development efforts.

## Planning Versus Strategy

The TSP approach makes no use of short-term, intermediate-
term, or long-term planning, as any of these are conventionally understood.  There is a strategy that provides a well-articulated
framework for decision making of all types, but no plan, as such.
The strategy provides a well-founded description of what should and
can be done, why it should be done, and where it will lead, and it
therefore provides an image of the way the region might appear,
were the strategy completely carried out.  But of course the strategy will not be completely carried out (that is a fact of the development setting), and so it does not feature a list of quantified interdependent target variables.  This is believed to be a major strength.
Additionally, the strategy part of the TSP approach minimizes the
use of formalized projections of any type and does not employ broad
optimization techniques in the commonly accepted mathematical sense.
Under the TSP approach, the overall strategy for the development of the region is merely the collection of strategies formulated
on the basis of specialized investigations for each of the various

aspects of the region's economic, social, and administrative activity. Those "sectoral" strategies spell out and justify the approach to be taken in order to bring about changes in line with the key strategy themes for each sector. Assembling them for presentation as the overall strategy for development involves a process of modification and adjustment, which should actually be an ongoing activity throughout step 2, to bring about their integration in light of sectoral interdependencies, time, space, national-setting, and policy considerations.

## Quantification

The TSP approach is not intended as a means of replacing quantitative analysis in general with qualitative judgments. It does, however, accept the latter as a legitimate alternative to the former when data are unreliable or when obtaining them involves an expenditure of planning resources that simply does not pay. The emphasis in the TSP approach is on forward movement, with increasingly detailed and final decisions made as reliable information becomes increasingly available and/or useful. It rejects the notion of an intensive expenditure of time, manpower, and money for data collection and quantitative analysis before plan formulation can get seriously under way. Clearly, however, quantitative techniques will have to be employed to some extent in dealing with impact assessment, and the aims of certain aspects of the overall strategy can only be expressed meaningfully in numerical terms.

Within the context of the TSP approach, quantification would be sought only where such quantification appears useful and meaningful in light of realities. In fact, those realities are rather harsh. We do not wish to get into the question of the reliability of even the "hardest" data usually found in developing countries, for Dudley Seers in his 1969 SID World Conference address, Gunnar Myrdal in Asian Drama, and others have already put in print what all of us who have ever worked with these data have known all along. Much of the quantification and mathematical modeling characteristic of current conventional planning is a luxury that is neither useful nor meaningful, even when it is thought "accurate," and may even impede more than hasten planning and development activity.

This may not be the case in the industrialized countries (though the matter is debatable), where the sources of conventional planning are ultimately found. The TSP approach suggests an alternative formulated with the features of the development setting in developing countries in mind, and we are increasingly, if belatedly, coming to realize the importance of such alternatives. In the context of

regional development in the Third World, target quantification and
the precise identification and quantification of behavioral links
(commonly through mathematical models) in any case probably will
not facilitate the decision-making process as it is practiced.

Some readers may feel that the diminished value and role assigned to quantitative techniques, while perhaps consistent with the
unconventionally "soft" orientation of the TSP approach, leaves
planners and decision makers without "objective" or "scientific"
bases for establishing priorities and measuring progress.  It would
be a mistake--and one more commonly made than not--to imagine
that, in general, quantification leads to objectivity or scientific
"solutions" in questions of regional development planning.  In such
questions, quantitative techniques are properly employed as supple-
ments to other methods, for they of necessity exclude the most important features of the development setting, such as culture, reli-
gion, history, tradition, national and local politics and government
policies, social values, the weather, the will of the people.  Nevertheless, the matters of priority setting and evaluation within the
"soft" TSP context must be addressed.

## Development Priority Setting

Allocation of development resources among alternative regional uses in developing countries most often is not a problem of
the same nature as is found in the industrialized countries, and
therefore the notion of priorities must be viewed in an entirely different light.  In developing countries, and particularly at the regional level, the problem is more to identify viable projects than to
choose among them.  Once a set of projects is identified, it will
usually be discovered that some "projects" will require no real
financing, because they involve matters of organization or improved
government operations that can be carried out through existing operating budgets, and most others will be candidates only for financing
from specific sources.  Thus, in reality, there will be very little
competition among projects for the same funds and, therefore, no
significant priority problem will exist.

When such competition does arise, it will usually be a matter
of selecting from among two or three specific project recommendations, and this can easily be handled without an elaborate mathematical overall priority-setting structure.  If the TSP approach is properly carried out, such a "microselection" problem should be readily
soluble by reference to the key strategy themes and the overall
strategy for the development of the region.

## Evaluation

If the foregoing paragraphs hold, it follows that measurement of progress must also be viewed differently, and certainly not in terms of a declining gap between actual and target values for selected indicators.  Since the key strategy themes specify only the desired directions of change and not the precise magnitudes, indicators providing measures of movement in those directions must serve, in the first instance, as the basis for evaluation of progress.  Their values may be compared with national norms, or with readings taken in the region at other points in time or with some other norm deemed appropriate.  But such indicators serve only in the first instance, and only if available in meaningful form.

Ultimately, under the TSP approach, progress must be gauged in terms reflecting the spirit of the approach.  Each time the TSP sequence is repeated, the process of determining key strategy themes and overall strategy for development becomes an evaluative activity.  How much progress has been made with regard to each?  Has what was formerly a "key" problem now become a residual one?  Have new factors appeared on the scene that make formerly marginal problems now matters of central urgency?  Has national policy altered in the interim in a way that requires revision of the key strategy themes and/or the overall strategy?  In short, how does the region look today, as pictured through the key strategy themes and overall strategy for development, compared with the previous image?  Given national values and development goals, are we satisfied, not with some quantified notion of the "progress" we have made but with the selection of themes that has guided us in our development work and with the way in which we have attempted to promote those themes?

## TSP and People

Owing to its relative "softness," the fact that recommendations are brought into focus step by step, and its field-activity nature, the TSP approach is uniquely suited to accounting for local values and reflecting the national setting.  Moreover, there is adequate room within the TSP context for a heavy reliance on citizen participation.  Development planning is a very serious business, whether "soft" or "hard":  It changes environments, ways of life, perhaps values, and patterns of social behavior.  It would be wrong to attempt to do so without the deepest possible involvement of those who are to be affected.  From the very first step the TSP practitioner will go astray if, with whatever good intentions, he attempts to analyze and plan for instead of with the people.

## Sequence and Substance

The TSP approach suggests a sequence of activities particularly suited to planning with an "activity/art" orientation and at the
same time accommodating coordination with "system/science"-
oriented planning at other levels (these terms are discussed at
length in the postscript).  The approach may tend to have the greatest appeal in areas where problems of data scarcity and reliability
are major, but it would be incorrect to view it principally as a
method for planning without data.  Like any other approach, this one
works best with a large amount of readily available reliable data.

The TSP approach does not produce a comprehensive plan, but
it does provide a comprehensive framework for planning, in that
each project recommended is seen within a total regional strategy,
and its implications for the regional key strategy themes can--and
should--be easily assessed.  Perhaps no less important is the fact
that the TSP approach provides a comprehensive framework for pre-
senting the recommendations of planners, the logic of which is easily
understood and evaluated by any official or community leader.  Furthermore, because the sequence of chapters of a planning report
could easily conform to the sequence of TSP steps, preparation of a
first rough draft of the report simultaneously with the progress of
planning work is facilitated by the approach.  However, the structure of a TSP planning report would be such that the likelihood of the
rejection of all planning work because of a single tactically unfortu-
nate conclusion or recommendation is lessened, since the tight interdependencies of a comprehensive formalized plan are absent.

Finally, as should by now be clear, the step-by-step TSP sequence carries major implications for the decision-making procedure
and for planning as a learning process.


## POSTSCRIPT

After publication of the first of the two articles on which the
foregoing was based, a large volume of relatively polarized reaction
came in.  This in itself was instructive, and, when grouped in accordance with their evaluations, an interesting if not surprising
categorization of the critics emerged.

First, there are those who spend the bulk of their professional
time engaged in practical regional planning activities in developing
countries.  Included are members of indigenous regional planning
teams, central government planning officials assigned to concentrate
all their efforts on a single region, certain Western planning consultants, and students from developing countries who have taken

leaves of absence from jobs of a field-practitioner nature to improve their work-related skills.

A second category of critics includes those who are not regularly involved with the practical field problems of regional development planning in developing countries, because their efforts are concentrated on broader administrative or theoretical issues, national-level planning problems, or regional development in the context of industrialized countries. Academic scholars, government officials dealing with research or planning on a national scale, consultants without significant experience in outlying regions of developing countries, and foreign assistance administrators who supplied comments fell into this category.

The former group of professionals tends to be concerned with the day-to-day problems of "selling" the region's interests to national authorities; getting a first-draft plan out in time for inclusion of some of the projects in the next year's national budget; arguing the case for detailed regional studies for which insufficient funds have been allocated; convincing the local elite to support the local development planning effort; avoiding actions, statements, and recommendations that would offend and anger the politically powerful; and so on. In short, this group tends to view regional development planning as an ongoing activity, perhaps closer to art than to science. That is a valid view, and it reflects the reality in which members of this group operate.

By contrast, the latter group of professionals tends to view regional development planning as a subsystem or subprocess of a national planning system or process. That, too, is a valid view, and it reflects this group's operating realities. Because they are dealing with planning problems of enormous scale, involving complex issues of aggregation, disaggregation, and coordination, and because there is a large body of literature recording experience and sophisticated techniques relevant to their work, these professionals have become accustomed to thinking very much in scientific terms.

Reaction to the TSP approach was generally favorable when it came from the activity/art group of critics, and unfavorable when it came from the system/science group of critics.

Most of us readily identify with either the activity/art or the system/science group described, and so we have been less than fully aware that a serious dichotomy of concerns prevails between them. Indeed, since virtually all the professional literature is generated and controlled by and for the system/science group, it is understandable that its members, in particular, in communicating with each other in print have the feeling that they are communicating with everyone professionally concerned with the field. Members of

the activity/art group who try to keep up with the literature often re-
mark that it somehow fails to address their most pressing concerns.

The simple fact appears to be that each of the groups continues
to ask and answer questions that remain of limited interest to the
other. At the risk of oversimplification, one might say that the
activity/art-ist is, above all, concerned with how to get things mov-
ing--fast--in his region and to keep them moving; the system/science-
ist is concerned primarily with the perfection of his system (planning,
budgeting, administrative, theoretical, and so on).

When confronted with the need to make a decision, the activity/
art-ist asks himself which course is likely to bring about the greatest material improvement in his region in the shortest possible time.
He is used to working under conditions of uncertainty and lack of information and expects some of what he promotes to be rejected or to
fail for other reasons. He is prepared to work pragmatically, starting with a general framework and getting down to more detailed spe-
cifics as progress is made, if it is made.

The system/science-ist, when confronted with the need to
make a decision, asks himself which course is most consistent with
the whole. He looks not only for internal consistency but for com-
pleteness. He seeks not only to deliver a finished product, but usually takes care to ensure that it will be accepted before it is delivered. He tends to be very disturbed by the rejection of any component of his system and will often be able more easily to come to
terms with the rejection of the whole. He seeks complete information and is very careful to state that the limitations of his system
are defined by the quantity and quality of information available to him.

When the concerns of planners generate a view of planning as a
system and science at one end and as an activity and art at the other,
one should not be surprised to find that effective regional planning
within an integrated national planning context usually remains a
fiction.

Of course, the dichotomy ought not and need not exist. A certain measure of flexibility and an appreciation for the tasks performed by their counterparts at other levels can bring about the com-
munication and productive cooperation between members of the two
groups necessary to integrate their efforts in a way that will enable
planning to make a greater contribution to development. Such flexibility and mutual appreciation can be encouraged through exchanges
of personnel among the various planning agencies and levels, socio-
bureaucratic adjustments, courses and conferences convened for the
purpose, and the development of a body of literature addressed to
the relevant issues.

CHAPTER

# 2

## THE REDUCED
## PLANNING APPROACH
## FOR REGIONAL
## DEVELOPMENT PROGRAMS
## IN LAGGING AREAS
Peter P. Waller

### THE NEED FOR REDUCED PLANNING

Problems of regional planning are steadily gaining more public attention in the developing countries. In the 1950s and 1960s
almost every country introduced national and sectoral development
plans. In the last years a multitude of regional plans, regional development institutions, and regional planning departments within the
national administration came into existence. So far as the development of regional planning is concerned, broadly three categories
can be distinguished:

1. Countries with a regional planning system (i.e., Iran and
Venezuela): The national territory is divided into planning regions,
the national development plan is regionalized, and the regional planning bodies have regional budgets and regional plans.
2. Countries with a national strategy for regional development (i.e., Peru): The national development plan is not regionalized, and there are regional plans and regional development authorities for special regions only. The national strategy, however, does
indicate certain regional priorities, growth poles, problem regions,
and so on.
3. Countries with neither a regionalized plan nor a national
strategy but only some vague ideas about certain priority regions,
mainly politically troubled or lagging regions: This remains typical
of the case in the vast majority of developing countries.

In both the second and third categories we find lagging regions
with no existing regional plans. Very often, governments see the
urgent need to develop these regions without being able to wait for

the creation of a regional planning system. Typically, either the
governments have simply started with some projects or they have
asked some consultants to prepare a comprehensive regional plan.
Both approaches have severe drawbacks.

Starting with some projects without a systematic regional analysis can be called the "trial-and-error" approach. Although the
projects from an isolated project-evaluation point of view may appear quite feasible, there is no guarantee that they are the key to the
development of the region, that the major bottlenecks of regional development are attacked through them. Also, quite commonly it is
realized after a short time that other complementary projects are
essential for the success of the original project, and so a host of un-
planned and costly additional measures becomes necessary. In many
countries the attitude of establishing regional planning institutions
for "complicated" advanced regions and leaving lagging regions with
isolated projects further aggravates regional dualism (which is not
only a question of money but also of top-level manpower), usually
concentrated in the advanced regions.

A last, but very serious, problem is the tendency to pin hopes
for the development of a lagging region on one big project (a dam,
irrigation, a modern highway, and so on). This is the easiest way
for the government to show how much it is interested in the development of such a region, since so much money is sacrificed for the
big project. In reality, this is just an alibi, because projects of
major magnitude are usually taken over by a foreign country, and
the government can then again forget the region in question--at least
until it turns out that the big project was not the key to development
of the region and, perhaps, even was a complete failure.

The other traditional approach to the problems of lagging regions is to ask some consultants to prepare a "comprehensive plan."
Since for such regions data are typically very scarce, a large team
will arrive and will work for some years until they finally present a
voluminous study. However, very often general conditions in the
country have changed so drastically in the meantime that the plan
will be praised by everyone but cannot serve as a basis for immediate action. Also, the whole approach of handing over a voluminous
plan is based on an erroneous concept of planning: Meaningful planning cannot end with the publication of a study but rather is a continuing process. Therefore, it is not surprising at all that even in
regions for which at some time a voluminous regional plan has been
published development is in reality concentrated on certain projects
(if anything), and the "plan" disappears in the drawers.

Thus, a new approach that tries to escape the drawbacks of
the two traditional approaches seems needed, if the deteriorating
political, social, and economic conditions in lagging regions are to

be counteracted.  The lessons of the past indicate that such a new approach should be judged according to the following criteria:  action orientation, reduction in analytical work, integration of program elements, flexibility of planning, and participation of the population.

After a short outline of one possible reduced planning approach it will then be judged according to these criteria.


## BASIC FEATURES OF THE REDUCED APPROACH

The reduced planning approach developed at the German Development Institute, Berlin, is the result of various consulting activities in lagging regions and consists mainly of a logical sequence of planning steps that lead to the identification of concrete projects and finally to the elaboration of an integrated regional development program (RDP).  In essence, then, it is a systematized, iterative search process for key projects in the development of a region, as it were a middle way between comprehensive planning and the trial-and-error approach (the steps are shown in Chart 2.1).


### Delineation of the Region

In some cases the study region is already clearly delineated, either in terms of administrative boundaries or in terms of a planning region.  Very often, however, only vague ideas in terms of a problem region exist, such as the "underdeveloped South," the "deteriorating mountain region," and so on.  In any case, the planner has to find out whether the strategy envisaged by the government can be successful within the given boundaries and how an action region in contrast to the given problem region should be delineated.

The point of departure in countries with a national strategy for regional development is the role that this strategy assumes for the study region.  Usually such terms as "core region," "upward transitional," "downward transitional," and so on are used.[1]  These types of region necessitate a certain regional development strategy, such as regional growth, concentration on infrastructure, fostering of social services, and so on.  Where this national strategy does not exist, the regional development strategy has to be deduced from general goals at the national level, interviews with decision makers, and so on (Goal Analysis I).

The next step is then a first evaluation of the problems and the development potential of the study region.  This first regional analysis can have the result that a larger action region with more potential has to be delineated (an example is given in the Madagascar case,

## CHART 2.1

### Planning Phases and Planning Steps

| Phases | Steps | "Entrances" |
|---|---|---|
| 1. Delineation of the region | 1.1 National strategy for regional development | Entrance I |
| | 1.2 Development potential | |
| | 1.3 Delineation | |
| 2. Regional analysis | 2.1 Population | |
| | 2.2 Economy | |
| | 2.3 Socio-political structure | |
| | 2.4 Factors of under-development | |
| 3. Goal analysis | 3.1 Identification of goals | |
| | 3.2 Development strategy | |
| 4. Sector and project analysis | 4.1 Selection of key sectors | Entrance II |
| | 4.2 Identification of key projects | Entrance III |
| | 4.3 Identification of support projects | |
| 5. Elaboration of RDP | 5.1 Construction of project complexes | |
| | 5.2 Spatial development concept | |
| | 5.3 Goal achievements of project complexes | |
| 6. Implementation of RDP | 6.1 Alternative implementation sequences | |
| | 6.2 Organizations for implementation | |
| | 6.3 Participation of population | |

Chapter 3). Another result can be that further investigations can be reduced to a smaller subregion (Kosi case, Chapter 5). In these cases various techniques of regional delineation can be applied. If, however, no change of given boundaries is possible and the envisaged strategy does not attack the problems of the region or is not matched by sufficient development potential, the planner should suggest another regional development strategy to the decision maker.

### Regional Analysis

After the planning region has been definitely delineated, a more detailed regional analysis can be undertaken as a next step in the iterative search process. A short overview of the various sectors is the basis for the selection of key sectors that will be investigated in detail. Thus, this regional analysis can be limited to basic information on the population structure, economic base of the region, and sociopolitical structure; no time-consuming comprehensive survey is necessary at this point. The result of this analysis should be a clear analysis of the factors of underdevelopment of the region that will be the basis for the judgment of the incidence of national goals and for the elaboration of a more detailed regional development strategy.

### Goal Analysis

Whereas in the first phase it is only possible to find out what the government thinks the regional development strategy should be, at this point a more detailed analysis of government goals at various levels, of goals of political groups, and of the felt needs of the population is necessary. Thereby a hierarchy of more general to more specific goals can be established, and goal conflicts can be uncovered. The subsequent theoretically desirable steps of goal operationalization and setting of clear priorities can in reality only be carried out for extremely limited fields (e.g., irrigation projects) but not for a region as a whole. On the other hand, a vague catalogue of goals cannot serve as the basis for the identification of projects.

The reduced approach, therefore, aims at concentration on a regional development strategy based on the major problem of the region. In lagging regions usually the potential is such a limiting factor that most groups will agree on a certain development strategy (see the Gwembe case, Chapter 6, on this problem). Based on this regional development strategy (e.g., regional growth through the

utilization of natural resources, expansion of social services, and
so on), existing goals can be grouped in priority goals that are
directly achieved through the strategy and nonpriority goals. The
latter will be used later as a "filter" when the goal achievements of
project complexes are evaluated.

### Sector and Project Analysis

On the basis of a regional-development strategy it is possible
to reduce the analysis of various sectors to certain key sectors (see
Chart 2.2) that are essential for the chosen development strategy.
The detailed analysis of those sectors leads to the identification of
key projects. A further study of the key projects then reveals that
other projects, called support projects, are essential for the success of the key projects. The support projects may be within the
same sector or within another sector not analyzed so far. Together
with their key project they form a project complex.

### Elaboration of RDP

After all project complexes have been identified, their spatial
interconnections through movements of goods, migrations of people,
and so on have to be studied (spatial development concept). In a
next step the goal achievements of the project complexes can be presented qualitatively in a goal-achievement matrix. This is not to
choose among various project complexes but rather to show certain
goal conflicts. Different constraints in terms of finance, experts,
and so forth are taken care of through alternative time sequences.

### Implementation of RDP

The most important steps for the implementation phase are the
establishment of the necessary regional organizations and the participation of the population. The RDP must include concrete proposals concerning how this can be achieved.

It is very important to understand the steps outlined above, not
as a rigid sequence but rather as a checklist leading to a concrete
RDP. Certain steps, such as goal analysis and regional analysis,
have to be undertaken several times, with different intensities.
Also, "entries" into the system are possible at different steps (see
Chart 2.1), but in each case all other steps should be undertaken,
as well. For example, if a certain project has already been

CHART 2.2

Identification of Projects

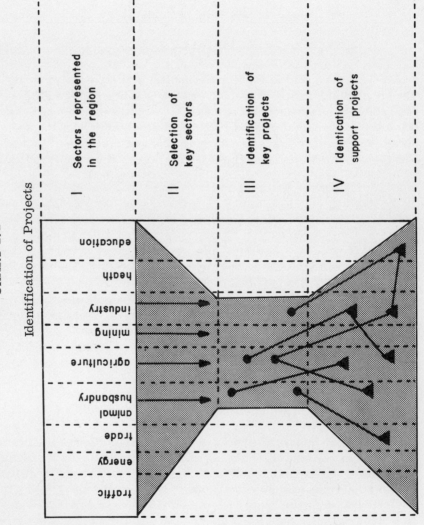

I    Sectors represented in the region

II   Selection of key sectors

III  Identification of key projects

IV   Identication of support projects

traffic
energy
trade
animal husbandry
agriculture
mining
industry
heath
education

designated for the planning region, an analysis of the national strategy, the regional development potential, and so on would be necessary to make sure that the project is indeed a key one for the development of the region.  This is the essential difference between the reduced planning approach and the trial-and-error approach.

## EVALUATION OF THE REDUCED PLANNING APPROACH

### Action Orientation

A planning approach can only be called action-oriented if the various administrations that have to implement it can understand and control it.  Complex scientific methods, such as input-output, shift analysis, location analysis, and so forth can and should be used to make certain details more precise, but they should never be an essential component of the planning process itself nor a necessary precondition for decisions.  Since the reduced planning approach is a rather simple but systemized search process, it is not dependent on a certain quality and amount of data and can therefore be applied even in rather backward areas.  The better the data, the more that quantitative methods can be applied, and the more precise are the results.  Typically, however, in lagging regions of developing countries the establishment of a body of regional data is a byproduct of the regional planning process itself.

Another basic aspect of action orientation is that the RDP must contain some implementable projects on which action can start immediately.  This does not mean, however, that all projects must be implemented at once.  Rather, these projects will show a varying degree of maturity; i.e., some will be at the level of proven feasibility, others on a prefeasibility level, and still others will just be project ideas.  This different degree of maturity can only be deplored by those who still see planning and implementation as two distinct and separable activities.  It also excludes any optimization of the RDP, because quantified goal contributions of the projects are only available after the last feasibility study is finished.  Even granted that all goal contributions would be quantifiable, the result of an optimization approach can only be that action on implementable projects has to be delayed for a long time and, when finally the last feasibility study is available, the data for the first study are already obsolete.  Therefore, such an approach is the exact opposite of action-oriented planning.

Reduction

In an RDP most of the time and manpower are consumed for the sector analysis and for feasibility studies. Usually, all sectors are analyzed and all information is collected without regard to its later usefulness. The reduced planning approach reduces work at three principal points: reduction of sectors, reduction of work within sectors, and elimination of feasibility studies from planning phase.

A drastic reduction of analytical work is only possible if the purpose for which data are needed is at least basically known. For a multiple-goals system, however, practically any data can be considered. Therefore, a reduction of the multiple-goal system is necessary before the major analytical work begins. A reduction of goals is also a sine qua non in lagging regions, because existing planning and evaluation methods with multiple goals are rather complicated and require excellent data. [2] The situation in lagging regions is not unlikely a war situation, where one overriding goal (victory) exists, and other goals have second priority only.

It seems clear that the identification of the overriding goal, or the basic development strategy as it is called in the reduced approach, requires a careful analysis of goals at various levels of society, including the felt needs of the local population. However, this is by far compensated through the reduction in sectors of investigation and in the collection of data. It is also essential that the result of the goal analysis of the planner is again discussed with decision makers and is supported by them.

Another aspect of goal reduction is that it is intensively linked to the evaluation of the development potential of the study region, because a certain development strategy is only feasible given a certain potential. What is required, therefore, is an iterative approximation between a range of nebulous, nonarticulated goals and a vaguely known development potential. The important aspect is not so much a strict sequence of steps but the assurance that all steps are included and planning work is minimized.

In lagging regions the reduced approach may lead to the reduction of sectors to but one, in many cases agriculture (an illustrative case of this situation is the Wollega region study described in Chapter 4) or to the reduction of projects to one single key project, such as the strategic road in the Kosi Zone (see Chapter 5). It is, however, important that this is either the result of the search process or at least supported by an analysis including the steps of the search process. This means that an "entrance" to the planning process is possible at various steps, but even if a certain sector or project is predetermined all other steps have to be analyzed as well (see Chart 2.1).

A last important reduction is the exclusion of detailed feasibility studies from the first round of the planning process leading to the RDP. This has to do with the understanding of planning. If one considers planning as the elaboration of a perfect, voluminous plan to be handed over to the decision maker at a very solemn moment, then indeed all projects must be on a feasibility level, because only feasible projects can be compared, and only final decisions about alternatives can be made. If one considers planning as a continuous incremental process, then certain decisions can be made based on projects in various degrees of maturity. After new information is available at a later time, new and correcting decisions can be made.

## Integration

First, the RDP has to be integrated into the national-planning framework. Second, projects and project complexes have to be integrated within the RDP itself. Both aspects are fully covered by the reduced approach outlined above. Integration into the national framework is achieved through an analysis of the national strategy for regional development in the very first step and through a detailed goal analysis. Within the regional analysis a central part is a detailed assessment of the region's links with the rest of the national territory (flow of goods, capital, labor, and so forth) and with other countries. The integration of key and support projects is realized within a project complex, whereas the links between project complexes are the subject of the spatial development concept.

## Flexibility

The essential aspect is that the implementation process is structured in such a way that new information and new data are fed back into the program as quickly as possible. Therefore, "decision thresholds" are proposed in the reduced approach (see the Madagascar case, Chapter 3). At certain time intervals all new information (feasibility reports, the result of pilot projects, the political situation, and so on) is evaluated in respect to the RDP. Then decisions about the continuation or change of existing projects, as well as the start of new projects, can be made.

Apart from basic adjustments of the RDP at decision thresholds, continuous flexibility is achieved through intraproject planning (an example is given in the Wollega case, Chapter 4). This means that the project management is given at least a minimum of decision-making power on the use of project funds. The advantage of intraproject planning is the principle of small circuits; i.e., information obtained in the course of project implementation is used directly for plan revision.

Another aspect of flexibility is that where great uncertainty exists, test or pilot phases should be planned before the actual project is started. This is especially important for projects where the motivation of the population and the implementation capacity of the administration play a decisive role. It is very difficult to judge those factors beforehand; in reality they can only be tried out. A good example for this is the point-line-network system used for agricultural projects (see the Wollega case, Chapter 4).

## Participation

Participation of the population is so essential for any type of regional planning that it certainly cannot be a field of reduction within the reduced approach. In industrialized countries there is now a strong desire on the part of planners to achieve citizen participation, and a variety of forms have been discussed. In developing countries participation is, however, even more important and more difficult, and there are many examples of technically and economically sound projects that failed because of lack of interest on the part of the population.

The reduced approach introduces participation at an early phase, that of goal analysis, where, in addition to the goals of the government, the felt needs of the population should be assessed. It is clear that for larger regions with a multiplicity of social groups scientific surveys are not possible within a short time period. Nevertheless, some indications can be obtained. The most critical aspect of citizen participation comes during the implementation phase, where general statements are not possible, since the forms of participation depend very much on the existing political and administrative structure of the region concerned. If, however, no participation of the population concerned seems feasible, the planner must ask himself whether he can justify the elaboration of an RDP.

## NOTES

1. Examples of various types of regions are given in J. Friedmann, Regional Development Policy: A Case Study of Venezuela (Cambridge, Mass.: M.I.T. Press, 1966), and R. A. Obudho and P. P. Waller, Periodic Markets, Urbanisation and Regional Planning--A Case Study from Western Kenya (Westport: Greenwood Press, 1976).

2. M. Hill and Y. Tzamir, "Multidimensional Evaluation of Regional Plans Serving Multiple Objectives," in Papers and Proceedings 29, Regional Science Association (1972), p. 140.

# 3

## THE APPLICATION
## OF A REDUCED
## PLANNING APPROACH:
## SOUTH MADAGASCAR

Peter P. Waller

This case study of South Madagascar is based on a report of the German Development Institute (GDI) to the German government at the request of the government of the Malagasy Republic.* After a preparatory mission in June 1973, the GDI study group stayed in Madagascar from November 1973 through January 1974. The study group's task was to identify possibilities for development aid in southern Madagascar on the basis of a regional development program (RDP). Typically, only limited time and manpower were available to work on the RDP; therefore, a reduced planning approach, elaborated previously at the GDI in collaboration with officials of the government, was used and thereby tested as to its practicability. (This approach and its planning steps are outlined in Chapter 2. The South Madagascar case follows Chart 2.1.) Because of the virtual absence of regional data, none of the more sophisticated methods of regional science could be applied. On the other hand, concrete projects had to be identified and a regional frame in the form of an integrated RDP had to be developed.

A final judgment of the applicability of the reduced approach can only be given after the proposed program has been implemented and possible shortcomings become evident. At the time of writing it can be said that it was possible to present results within a year from the beginning of the preparatory mission, and that concrete

---

*Deutsches Institut für Entwicklungspolitik, Ein regionales Entwicklungshilfe-Programm für die Südwest-Region Madagaskars, Vol. A, "Konzept und Ergebnisse," Vol. B, "Regional- und Sektoranalysen," 6 vols. (Berlin: [German Development Institute], 1974).

# MAP 3.1

## Location and Delineation of Planning Region

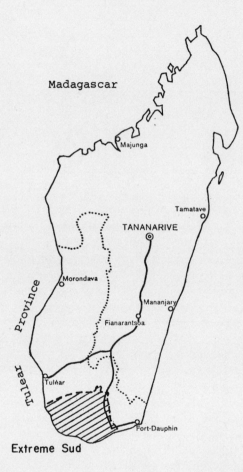

Madagascar

Majunga

Tamatave

TANANARIVE

Morondava

Mananjary

Fianarantsoa

Tuléar

Fort-Dauphin

Province

Tulear

Extreme Sud

 planning region
Tulear

 program region
Southwest

 problem region
"Extreme sud"

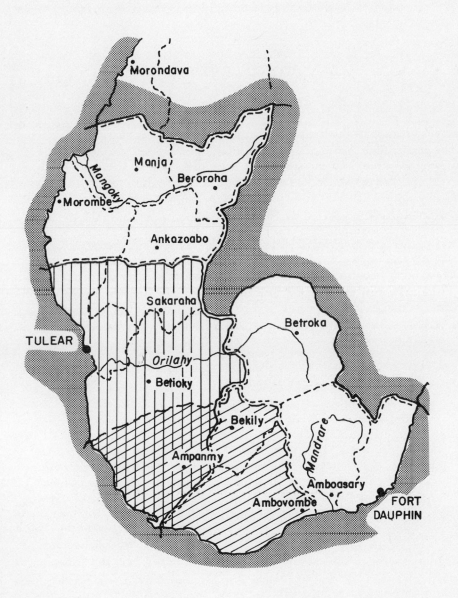

Morondava

Manja
Beroroha
Mangoky
Morombe

Ankazoabo

Sakaraha
Betroka

TULEAR
Orilahy
Betioky

Bekily
Mandrare

Ampanmy
Amboasary

Ambovombe
FORT
DAUPHIN

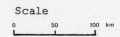

Scale

0        50        100  km

33

negotiations between the two governments on the basis of these results have been initiated. Since the situations in many lagging regions in developing countries seem to be similar to that in South Madagascar, the approach presented here is likely to be applicable in many cases.

## DELINEATION OF THE REGION

### National Strategy for Regional Development

The Malagasy Republic belongs to the group of developing countries that have not yet developed a definite national strategy for regional development. After political uprisings in the South in 1971 this part of the country, certainly a lagging region, was given first priority for development. An Interministerial Commission (Working Group XII) that was set up after the events of 1971 drew up preliminary proposals for development based on a growth strategy through the exploitation of regional resources. Some of the projects identified by this group were not feasible, and a program for immediate action was not proposed. Moreover, the delineation of the region was not clear and an integrated concept was not given. However, there was no doubt that the new government that took over in 1972 still gave the South high priority and wanted development through the exploitation of resource potentials.

### Level of Development and Development Potential

Initially, the "South" was considered to encompass the province of Tulear (see Map 3.1). An analysis of the level of development of the South is rather difficult, since in the Malagasy Republic no regionalized data on per capita income are available. A study of the year 1960 puts the average income per inhabitant in some subprefectures of the South at $13 to $16, whereas the national average for rural incomes was $33. In terms of social indicators, the South is last in the list of Madagascar's six provinces (see Table 3.1).

The level of development within Tulear Province varies to a great degree. The extreme sud (Extreme South) may be defined as the real distressed area (see Map 3.1). The insurgence in 1971 was concentrated there, and the level of development indicators reach their lowest rates in this area. For instance, the school enrollment rate in the subprefecture of Ampanihy is only 22.0, as compared to 35.1 for the province and 48.8 for the whole country. The number of inhabitants per doctor (in thousands) is 25.6, as against 23.7 for the province and 10.4 for the country (see Table 3.1).

TABLE 3.1

Ranking of Provinces by Social Indicators, 1972

| Province | Enrollment Rate (thousands) | Ranking | Inhabitant/doctor (thousands) | Ranking | Inhabitant/hospital bed (thousands) | Ranking |
|---|---|---|---|---|---|---|
| 1. Tananarive | 58.7 | 1 | 5 | 1 | 362 | 1 |
| 2. Diego-Suarez | 54.7 | 2 | 11 | 2 | 418 | 2 |
| 3. Majunga | 53.0 | 3 | 12 | 3 | 491 | 3 |
| 4. Tamatave | 51.7 | 4 | 16 | 4 | 522 | 6 |
| 5. Fianarantsoa | 40.1 | 5 | 23 | 5 | 521 | 5 |
| 6. Tulear | 35.1 | 6 | 24 | 6 | 493 | 4 |
| Madagascar | 48.8 | | 10 | | 433 | |

Sources: Enrollment rate: Ministere de l'Education Nationale et des Affaires Culturelles, Situation de l'enseignement (Tananarive, 1972), p. 12. Inhabitant/doctor; inhabitant/hospital bed: Second Development Plan (unpublished), Ch. 65, p. 2; Service Provincial de la Sante, Tulear 1974.

As the terms of reference of the Malagasy government only referred in general to the "South," the need for a precise demarcation arose at the very outset. The problem region Extreme South was first delineated by applying the level of development criteria. The area in question is more or less identical with the region inhabited by the Mahafaly and Antandroy tribes and is characterized by very low (less than 60 centimeters per year) precipitation (see Map 3.1).

A preliminary regional analysis of this problem region showed the development potential to be very limited--that is, the prerequisites for a growth strategy based on utilization of natural resources as envisaged in the national strategy were not present. Because of the low and irregular rainfall and the marginal soils, the possibility of promoting crop farming was minimal in comparison to the other regions of Madagascar. Animal husbandry, the most important economic activity, had already reached its limits, as evident from acute overgrazing combined with soil erosion. A structural change in traditional cattle raising was, at the most, possible in the long term. The only known mineral resources were rather large kaolin deposits; no preconditions for industrialization existed.

Given this situation, it was decided to see whether the region could be expanded to include areas with higher potential so that a growth strategy for the whole enlarged region would become feasible. A regional analysis of Tulear Province disclosed that considerable resources were available in agriculture (irrigation and new pastures) and in mining (coal, limestone, and bauxite), and that the opportunities for industrialization were present, especially in the town of Tulear.

Delineation of the Planning Region

As a result of the foregoing analysis, the planning region for the implementation of the envisaged regional-development strategy had to encompass the problem region Extreme South, as well as the future growth center Tulear. The precise delineation of the planning region was therefore based on the limits of the hinterland of Tulear. Fortunately, a detailed empirical study based on such functional criteria as hinterland of Tulear banks, wholesale trade, transport enterprises, and so forth already existed. After considering other factors, such as existing administrative boundaries and future trends, the planning region was delineated, covering most of Tulear province with the exception of some northern subdistricts (see Map 3.1).

For reasons of "division of labor" with other institutions working in Southern Madagascar the GDI team confined its activities to
one of the three subregions, the program region Southwest (see Map
3.1).


## REGIONAL ANALYSIS

### Population

The total population of the program region Southwest amounted
to 336,000 on January 1, 1972; the population density was 7.6 inhabitants per square kilometer and was far below the national average (see Table 3.2).  The population is very unevenly distributed
within the program region--a fact that is closely related to the different climatic and topographical conditions.  The most densely
populated areas (more than ten inhabitants per square kilometer)
are to be found in the Onilahy Valley and around Tulear, where arti-
ficial irrigation is possible.  The main areas of outmigration are
the southern coastal strip and the Ampanihy area (see Map 3.1).
This is a temporary migration with the clear aim of returning to the
home village later.  The immigration areas in the South are the
Mangoky region, Tulear, and the Mandrare area (see Map 3.1).
However, the majority of the people migrate to the centers in the
plateau and the plantations in the north of Madagascar--distances of
more than 1,000 kilometers.


TABLE 3.2

Area and Population of the Program Region
Southwest, January 1, 1972

| Subprefecture | Area (sq. km.) | Population | Pop./sq. km. |
|---|---|---|---|
| Tulear | 5,878 | 112,712 | 16.4 |
| Sakaraha | 8,865 | 44,748 | 5.0 |
| Betioky | 15,214 | 102,014 | 6.7 |
| Ampanihy | 13,306 | 76,907 | 5.8 |
| Program region | 44,263 | 336,381 | 7.6 |
| Tulear province | 164,290 | 1,135,561 | 6.9 |
| Madagascar | 589,586 | 7.705,086 | 13.1 |

Source: Office de la Recherche Scientifique et technique Outre-
Mer, ORSTOM-MDR, Conditions geographiques de la mise en valeur
agricole, vol. 5 (Paris Tananarive:  Ministere du Developpement
Rural, n.d.), p. 40.

Economic Structure and Development Potential

The location of the Southwest region may be termed unfavorable with respect to the consumption and production centers of Madagascar.  Next to Diego-Suarez in the North, Tulear is the provincial capital situated at the greatest distance from Tananarive. On the other hand, the location on the sea is a positive factor, particularly as the region has a very good natural harbor in Tulear that is only used to 25 percent of its capacity, whereas Tamatave, Madagascar's largest port, is constantly congested.  The port of Tulear has the potential to serve as a supraregional port for the southern part of the plateau (from Fianarantsoa to Antsirabe).

The region's exports consist almost exclusively of agricultural products, either in an unprocessed or in a processed form.  International exports are mostly made up of meat from the Tulear meat factory, peas, fish, and, to a lesser degree, lobsters.  Of the cattle sold in the region about 25,000 are processed annually in the meat factory, but the same number are driven to the plateau and the east coast to be slaughtered, partly for overseas export.  Peas (pois de cap) are sent unprocessed principally to England and are canned there.

The principal commodities supplied to other parts of Madagascar are cooking oil, cotton, live animals, hides, and fish.  Cooking oil is manufactured in the oil mill at Tulear from peanuts and cottonseed grown in the region.  Regionally produced cotton is cleaned in a gin; the seed is sent to the oil mill, but the fibers are delivered for further processing to the textile factory in Antsirabe on the plateau.

The foreign trade structure of the Southwest region displays all the typical weaknesses characterizing the foreign trade of developing countries:  Primary commodities are exported; processed products are imported; employment in the processing industries is mainly created in other regions.

Apart from the development possibilities in processing industries, the important potential of the region is found in agriculture, mining, and industrialization based on mining.

The development potential in dry-farming agriculture is limited to certain areas with good soils and precipitation of more than 600 meters.  A considerable expansion of irrigated areas is possible in the Onilahy Valley.  An increase in livestock production can only be envisaged in the long term, due to the poor quality of the pastures and the difficulties in introducing modern techniques, described below.

The region possesses considerable mineral resources that have not yet been exploited.  The Sakoa coal field near Betioky is the only large-scale coal deposit in Madagascar; kaolin is found near

Ampanihy, and lime and clay near Soalara south of Tulear.   More
detailed studies will be required to ascertain whether there is sufficient foundation for profitable mining activities and the establishment
of related industry, such as cement factories, iron smelting, carbochemicals, and so on.  Along the coast fishing in outrigger boats is
an important activity; in some places lobsters and shrimps are also
caught.  The findings of an FAO research ship indicate, however, that
there is no major potential.

Tourism is poorly developed and has declined greatly in comparison to rates during the colonial era.  The region certainly possesses scenic tourist attractions, such as the Onilahy Canyon, the
Isalo mountains, the sand beaches, the coral reefs.  In the foreseeable future, however, other areas more favorably located for
European tourists will attract the major share of the low-volume
tourism in Madagascar.  The establishment of relations with South
Africa would, of course, immediately give the Southwest an advantage with respect to South African tourists.

The only location for future industrialization in the region is
the town of Tulear.  There, three industrial enterprises are already
located (meat factory, oil mill, and cotton gin), with some expansion
potential (meat factory) and some potential linkages (textile industry).
The location of a cement factory based on lime and coal would be at
Soalara, only 20 miles south of Tulear.  The infrastructure is very
good insofar as the port is concerned and has to be improved insofar
as the road connection to the plateau is concerned.  Thus, Tulear is
the only location in the South that offers possibilities for agglomera-
tion economies.  Therefore, it has also some potential for import-
substitution industries and regional industries that might raise incomes in the region.

In principle it may be said that a long-term evolution of a
growth pole in Tulear is certainly feasible.  Prerequisites are government measures to improve infrastructure and to implement various industrial and mining projects.


Sociopolitical Structure

The most important tribes in the Southwest region are the
Mahafaly, the Antanosy, the Bara, and the Vezo.  Similar to the
other coastal peoples of Madagascar, these tribes have a common
African origin, whereas the tribes on the plateau, particularly the
Imerina, immigrated from Indonesia.

The tribes in the South have the traditional form of society,
concerning which four main features should be mentioned.  First,
the "monolithic structure" is manifested by the power vested in the

head of the extended family who makes economic decisions and even has the right to command the savings of returned migrants. Cattle are the most important symbol of social prestige and wealth. At the same time they serve as savings and social security. The essential factors are the number of animals and the shape of their horns. Second, the cult of the dead orients the whole life of a man toward the preparation for death. The financial expenditure for an expired person (stone, tomb and death rites) can bring ruin to the remaining family members. A third obstacle to modernization of the South is to be found in the widespread taboos (fadys). For instance, some farmers refuse to irrigate their fields, others will keep no sheep, and so forth. In addition to the obstacles stemming from the traditional structure of society, a psychological/political barrier also plays a role in the South--namely, a deep-rooted aversion to government administration (fanjakana). From the historical point of view it was the South that offered the longest resistance to the expansion of the Imerina Kingdom. The replacement of Imerina rule by the French colonial administration hardly improved the situation of the people, as taxes had to be paid by Southerners, while the money was expended mainly in the plateau and the North.

In the recent past the government has been making an effort to encourage greater participation of the people in local decisions by reviving the fokonolona, a precolonial self-administration system. Fokonolona is the village assembly where each person has freedom of expression and where decisions have to be taken unanimously after a lengthy opinion-building process. On this foundation the government envisages a five-step system ranging from the village assembly to the provincial council. The fokonolona system is also intended to neutralize the traditional parties that continue to have influence in Madagascar even after the assumption of power by General Ramanantsoa's regime in May 1972. In the South, apart from the Parti Social-Democrat (PSD), the former government party, a regional party, the Mouvement National pour l'Independance de Madagascar (MONIMA), plays an important role. It was the moving force of the spring 1971 revolt that was suppressed by the PSD government. The MONIMA advocates the socialization of production means and a redistribution of land. As it is fundamentally opposed to government administration and to foreign experts, its influence should be taken into consideration when development measures are planned.

### Reasons for Underdevelopment

In summation, the findings of the regional analysis give the following main reasons for underdevelopment in the South:

1. Natural resources: In the agricultural-production sector resources are limited, due to low precipitation and poor soils; in the mining sector sizable deposits could not be exploited economically up to the present.

2. Economic structure: Only a small part of the market commodities produced (cattle, peanuts, cotton, peas, and rice) is processed in the region; the greater share is sent to other parts of Madagascar or is exported overseas, either wholly unprocessed (live cattle and peas) or with some preliminary processing (cotton).

3. Sociopolitical structure: In the South the influence of the traditional society (status of cattle, cult of the dead, and so on is much more powerful than it is in other parts of Madagascar; due to historical events, the attitude of the population toward government bodies is one of animosity.

4. Government policy in the past: Up to now the policy of the central government vis-a-vis the South was marked by great neglect; investment in infrastructure and promotion of industry mainly benefited the central plateau and the northern part of Madagascar.

GOAL ANALYSIS

Identification of Goals

The basis of the national goal system in Madagascar is the 1971 "Charte de Developpement," which was later supplemented by the Second Development Plan of 1972-74. The main general goals are "improvement of living conditions," "economic independence," and "more equitable distribution of national resources." In a policy statement made by the head of state on August 31, 1973, another main goal was added: maitrise populaire, the participation of the entire population in the shaping of political, economic, and social life.

From numerous talks with members of the government and from their interpretations it was possible to derive a "goal hierarchy" and, finally, a list of more specific and articulate goals (see Table 3.3). It is self-evident that some goals will overlap (e.g., $G_4$ and $G_5$); others will be mutually conflicting (e.g., $G_3$ and $G_4$ or $G_6$ and $G_7$); yet others will form the prerequisites for other goals. Obviously, we were not dealing with a clear-cut hierarchy of main and subsidiary goals but a complex goal system that had not been operationalized or weighted at the national level by the Malagasy side.

TABLE 3.3

National Catalogue of Goals with Respect to the
Development of the South

| Goal | Priority | Nonpriority |
|---|---|---|
| 1.  Improvement of health | | $G_1$ |
| 2.  Improvement of education | | $G_2$ |
| 3.  Creation of income | $G_3$ | |
| 4.  More equitable distribution of income | | $G_4$ |
| 5.  Reduction of regional disparities | $G_5$ | |
| 6.  Reorientation to the inland market | | $G_6$ |
| 7.  Diversification of exports | | $G_7$ |
| 8.  Direct participation in economic activities | | $G_8$ |
| 9.  Domestic capital formation | | $G_9$ |
| 10.  Use of regional resources | $G_{10}$ | |
| 11.  Regional integration | $G_{11}$ | |
| 14.  Adequate structures for participation | $G_{14}$ | |
| 15.  Application of adapted techniques | | $G_{15}$ |

Note:  Goals $G_{12}$ and $G_{13}$ are subsumed under $G_5$ and $G_{11}$
respectively.

Identification of Regional Development Strategy

The strategy paper prepared by the Interministerial Working
Group XII outlined a regional development strategy for the South of
Madagascar, in which the exploitation of natural resources is intended as the principal generator of regional growth.  (The reader
may find it helpful to refer back to Chart 2.1.)  The preference for
a "natural-resources" strategy to develop the South is a clear decla-
ration, in comparison to the complex and vague statements on goals.
Discussions with national and regional decision makers disclosed
that this strategy was clearly supported, and there was no mention of
other alternatives.  Apart from this, it also appeared to be certain
that the most important social group in the South outside the government, the MONIMA, was prepared to support such a strategy, even
though its objectives in doing so were quite different from those of
the government.

A regional growth strategy has two components:  export increase and import substitution programs.  The natural resources
strategy indicates a concentration on production for export.  This

seems to be justified in the case of South Madagascar, as the market for import substituting industrialization (e.g., the beverages industry) is still too small, and import substitution in the trade and service sectors has already taken place.

On the basis of a natural resources strategy the identified goals can be divided into priority goals (i.e., those that can be attained directly by this strategy) and nonpriority goals (see Table 3.3). It is important that this type of strategy also attack the factors of underdevelopment derived from the regional analysis. Only the third reason, the antagonistic attitude of the population toward government administration, is not directly influenced by this development strategy. On the contrary, a change in that attitude is an essential prerequisite for its success. The only possibility of modifying that negative attitude seems to be a stronger participation of the people in all measures--e.g., within the framework of the fokonolona system. For this reason the application of a growth strategy means that "participation" (see Table 3.3) must be added to the priority goals.

## SECTOR AND PROJECT ANALYSIS

The regional analysis showed that unused natural resources could be found in agriculture, livestock, mining, and the port of Tulear. These were therefore identified as key sectors for a regional-growth strategy based on the use of natural resources. Another key sector to be analyzed was industry, where some of these natural resources could be further processed. Other sectors, such as fishery, forestry, tourism, and infrastructure, could be eliminated as key sectors.

### Identification of Key Projects

In the agricultural sector analysis was concentrated on dry farming, livestock, and irrigation. Before production in dry farming can be expanded it is necessary to overcome the labor bottleneck that occurs during the tilling and ploughing seasons. The introduction of an ox-drawn plough would make a vital contribution; this, however, implies improved animal husbandry, intensive agricultural extension, creation of a repair service for ploughs, and so on. Therefore, the solution is an integrated rural development project ($P_{11}$).* Due to the intensity of the measures, all farms cannot be

---

*The numbers of the projects refer to Chart 3.1.

covered at the same time, so a point-line-network system will be
required. (This system will be explained more fully in Chapter 4.)
In keeping with Malagasy terminology, three agricultural development
zones (zone d'expansion rurale: ZER) were proposed. These in turn
were divided into subzones (secteur d'expansion rurale: SER). The
following procedure is envisaged for the system: In a pilot SER in
the Fotadrevo ZER a three-year preimplementation or test program
will be carried out; as soon as success is visible, a pilot SER in each
of the other two development zones will be launched; after about five
years the new techniques should have gained so much ground in the
pilot SER that the majority of the extension workers and the funds
can be withdrawn and utilized in another subzone of the same development zone.

    Meat production can be increased in the long term by improving
pastures ($P_{22}$) and veterinary services ($P_{21}$). The pasture area of
Mikoboka could serve as a reserve area for pastures in the Ampanihy
area, which need to be regenerated. Far-reaching project concepts,
such as the proposal made by a consulting firm to set up big ranches
or to introduce a large-scale triangular system (breeding of cattle in
the Mahafaly area--fattening in the Betroka area--slaughter in
Tulear), proved to be impracticable after detailed analyses.

    In the Onilahy Valley several additional irrigation areas total-
ing 12,000 hectares were identified; their internal rate of return can
be considered satisfactory by both national and international standards. However, exploitation of these areas will require the creation of a uniform organization (River Valley Authority) and the solution of difficult problems in the sociocultural field (antagonistic attitude of the population toward agricultural extension workers, conflicts between the settled population and migrants, clarification of
land laws, and so forth). Before the implementation of large-scale
projects can be contemplated, satisfactory solutions have to be found
for the present irrigation projects ($P_3$).

    The principal mineral resources of the region--coal, kaolin,
and limestone--are already the subject of intensive studies conducted
by private firms of consulting engineers at the request of the government. It is, however, important to remember that the economic exploitation of minerals and the creation of industrial projects based
on minerals (cement factory, thermal power plant, steel industry,
carbochemicals, and so on) are only feasible if there is a jointly used
infrastructure, such as the joint port installations in Soalara near
Tulear, common railway lines, and so forth. After the studies on
the individual minerals have been completed, a feasibility study on
an integrated heavy-industry complex should be commissioned ($P_5$).

    The main reason why the port of Tulear has little supraregional
importance and remains unused as an export base with several hundred

additional jobs, lies in the fact that the traffic links to the plateau are inadequate and uncertain. To utilize the potential of the port of Tulear, no key project was necessary; rather, two support projects in the traffic sector were identified.

In the industrial sector four projects were identified. First, there should be an expansion of the capacity of the meat factory. The precondition is that the live animals (5,000 to 10,000 head) exported via Fort Dauphin in the past should be processed, and the quota reserved for the Tulear factory should be raised so that fewer cattle will be sent from the South to other meat factories. Second, there should be a textile factory ($P_{42}$). In the first phase there would be substitution of raw cotton exports by cotton textile exports (feasibility study). Third, there should be an assembly unit ($P_{41}$), producing agricultural machinery, tractors, and small transporters. A shifting of agricultural machinery production from Tananarive is already envisaged (feasibility study). Finally, there should be a tannery ($P_{43}$). Exports of raw hides can be substituted by crust-leather exports. Approximately half of the required raw material could be supplied by the meat factory (feasibility study).


### Identification of Support Projects

For the integrated rural-development project three support projects are necessary (see Map 3.2). The first is the Ambatry-Bekily road ($P_{12}$), which opens up the Fotadrevo pilot SER and also links the Betroka-Isoanola area to Tulear. It must be improved so that it will be an all-weather road. The second project is the bilharzia campaign ($P_{13}$). Bilharziasis is widely prevalent in the Fotadrevo region and leads to a great loss in labor productivity. By utilizing the infrastructure required for $P_{11}$ a specialist in tropical diseases should introduce measures to control it and also to carry out tests to destroy the intermediate hosts of the disease. The third is the village artisan school ($P_{14}$). A village artisan school has to be built at an early stage so that the repair workshops set up after the introduction of the plough under $P_{11}$ can be transferred to independent artisans.

For the port of Tulear two support projects were identified. The first is the Sakaraha-Ankaramena road ($P_{48}$). This part of National Highway 7 between Tulear and Tananarive is not asphalted. It has to be improved, and in a second phase it should be asphalted. The other is the Tulear-Tanandava road ($P_{47}$). The necessary improvement of this road would direct most of the export of the growing Mangoky region from the uneconomic small port of Morombe to the port of Tulear.

MAP 3.2

Location of Project Complexes

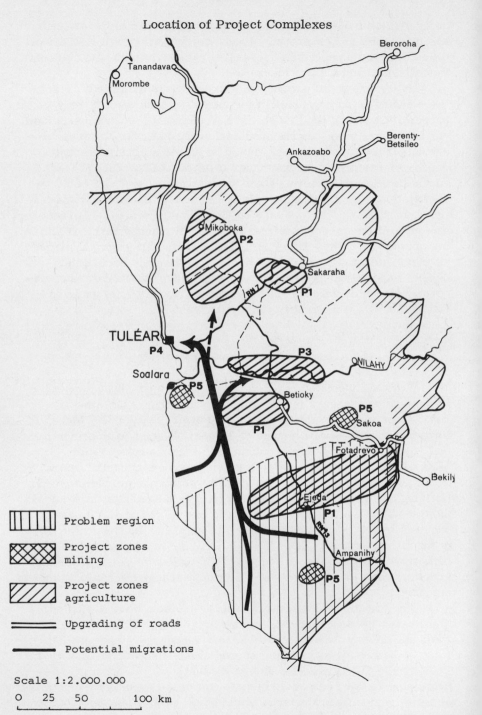

For the industrial development of Tulear three support projects were identified. The first concerns the selection of industrial sites ($P_{45}$). The areas officially earmarked for future industries in Tulear are mainly swamps. Suitable land has been identified, but a technical study on the opening up of the area and the organization of an industrial zone will have to be undertaken. The second concerns the Sakaraha-Beroroha road ($P_{46}$) and the Tulear-Tanandava road ($P_{47}$). The largest reserves for the increase of cotton production lie in the Mangoky region. In the Beroroha area, in particular, the extension of the cultivation area is dependent on a better road network, so this project is an important precondition for the construction of a textile factory in Tulear. The third concerns National Highway 7 ($P_{48}$), which has to be upgraded to a reliable all-weather road between Sakaraha and Ankaramena for there to be an expansion of industry in Tulear.

Other support projects were identified that make a positive contribution to the key projects but that are not directly linked to a particular key project alone. For instance, a radio station in Tulear ($S_1$) would play an important role in mobilizing and educating the farmers within the framework of the integrated rural development project $P_{11}$. Its importance extends further, however, because a greater mobilization of the population is needed for the establishment of the fokonolona self-administration system.

After the key and support projects were identified they were grouped to form complexes. Project complex $P_4$ (the growth pole Tulear, for example) combines the subsectors port and industry, as both are closely linked to one another and are related to the same location, Tulear.

## FORMULATION OF THE RDP

### Spatial Development Concept

The salient features of the spatial-development concept can be understood best by reference to Map 3.2. The starting point is the realization that the potential of the problem area (subprefecture Ampanihy) does not suffice to provide all its inhabitants with additional income. The available resources in the agricultural and mining sectors are to be utilized to the full (programs $P_1$ and $P_5$), but additional income will be confined to a few privileged areas or will be generated in the growth pole Tulear-Soalara.

The concept, therefore, intentionally includes intraregional migration. It is held that migration within the region--i.e., over a distance of 100 to 300 kilometers--is of a different quality than that

of migration over distances exceeding 1,000 kilometers. In the former the contact to the home village is preserved: It can be visited
once a year at least and also if particular occasions, such as the
death of a relative, arise. An interview of the workers in Tulear
revealed that the migrants partly help in agriculture, invest in agricultural machinery, introduce improvements, and so on. All this
would hardly be possible in the case of interregional migration, or
it would at least involve considerably higher costs.

     If intraregional migration is accepted as an instrument of re-
gional development, it must be used in a planned and systematic man-
ner--i.e., an attempt must be made to create suitable employment
for migrants within the region. In the Southwest the employment
opportunities in question are jobs as settlers in the Onilahy irrigation project and industrial jobs in industry and the services sector in
the Tulear/Soalara growth pole. As the number of possible migrants
to the Onilahy (program $P_3$) is put at a maximum of 4,500 in the next
ten years (and it will probably be lower, if other constraints, especially of a social nature, are taken into consideration), it becomes
evident that the expansion of Tulear into a growth pole is a central
issue, as it is there that the workplaces have to be created for migrants from the problem area. The basis for this expansion is provided by programs $P_4$ (processing of agricultural products and establishment of an assembly unit) and $P_5$ (establishment of a heavy-
industry complex in Soalara based on mining), which will enable the
creation of about 2,000 to 3,000 direct workplaces in industry and at
least as many jobs in the tertiary sector.

### Goal Achievements of Project Complexes

     A glance at Table 3.4 shows that all project complexes can
make positive contributions to the priority goals. In the field of nonpriority goals two fundamental goal conflicts, indicated in Table 3.4
by minus signs, arise. First, none of the project complexes achieves
the goal "more equitable distribution of income within the region."
By concentrating the projects in the high-potential zones, an intraregional income disparity is intentionally created in order to induce
the inhabitants of low-potential areas to migrate. This is the well-
known goal conflict in regional planning between the reduction of
interregional and intraregional differences in income. In order to
decrease regional disparities at the national level (goal $G_5$) the income of lagging regions must be raised as a whole, and this can only
be done by concentrating on the high-potential areas in those regions.
If, for instance, in the development of a lagging region priority would
be given to the goal of equitable intraregional distribution (therefore

promoting agriculture in all areas), the financial resources and available skilled labor would not be ensured even in the privileged areas. At a later phase, when the regional development process is operating smoothly and financial resources are not needed to the same extent in the privileged areas, more weight could be given to social programs within the framework of the RDP.

TABLE 3.4

Goal Contribution of the Project Complexes

| Goals | $P_1$ Rural Development | $P_2$ Livestock Improvement | $P_3$ Irrigation | $P_4$ Growth Pole Tulear | $P_5$ Heavy Industry |
|---|---|---|---|---|---|
| **Priority goals** | | | | | |
| $G_3$ Creation of income | ++ | + | ++ | ++ | ++ |
| $G_5$ Reduction of regional disparities ($G_{12}$) | + | | + | ++ | ++ |
| $G_{10}$ Use of regional resources | ++ | + | + | | ++ |
| $G_{11}$ Regional integration of Madagascar | | | + | ++ | ++ |
| $G_{14}$ Participation | + | | + | | |
| **Nonpriority goals** | | | | | |
| $G_1$ Improvement of health | + | | | | |
| $G_2$ Improvement of education | + | | | + | |
| $G_4$ More equitable distribution of income | − | | − | − | − |
| $G_6$ Reorientation to the inland market | + | | + | | |
| $G_7$ Diversification of exports | | + | | | + |
| $G_8$ Direct participation in economic activities | + | + | + | +− | − |
| $G_9$ Domestic capital formation | + | + | + | +− | − |
| $G_{13}$ Application of adapted techniques | + | | | | − |

# CHART 3.1

## Schedule for Implementation of Development Projects
### (Costs in $1,000)

| Designation of Project | Alternative I | | | | | | Costs |
|---|---|---|---|---|---|---|---|
| | 0 1974 | 1 1975 | 2 1976 | 3 1977 | 4 1978 | 5 1979 | |
| $P_{11}$ Rural Pilot Project | | | | | | | 1.000 |
| $P_{12}$ Ambatry-Bekily Road | | | | | | | 25 |
| $P_{13}$ Bilharzia Campaign | | | | | | | 320 |
| $P_{14}$ Village Artisan School | | | | | | | 380 |
| $P_{21}$ Veterinary Service | | | | | | | |
| $P_{22}$ Pasture Areas Study | | | | | | | 120 |
| $P_{31}$ Irrigation Onilahy | | | | | | | |
| $P_{41}$ Assembly Unit Study | | | | | | | 45 |
| $P_{42}$ Textile Factory Study | | | | | | | 50 |
| $P_{43}$ Tannery Study | | | | | | | 40 |
| $P_{44}$ Groundnut Shelling Study | | | | | | | 15 |
| $P_{45}$ Industrial Area Study | | | | | | | 25 |
| $P_{46}$ Sakaraha-Beroroha Road | | | | | | | 300 |
| $P_{47}$ Tulêar-Tanandava Road | | | | | | | 150 |
| $P_{48}$ National Highway 7 | | | | | | | |
| $P_{49}$ CET (Instead of $P_{14}$) | | | | | | | (290) |
| $P_5$ Heavy Industry Study | | | | | | | 700 |
| $S_1$ Radio Station | | | | | | | 450 |
| $S_2$ Verne Station | | | | | | | 10 |
| $S_3$ Medicines | | | | | | | 520 |
| $S_4$ BDPI | | | | | | | 15 |
| Costs of all projects | 80 | 370 | 520 | 1.500 | 950 | 525 | 4.145 |

——————  Project Costs (Estimate possible)

- - - - - - -  Project Costs (Estimate not yet possible)

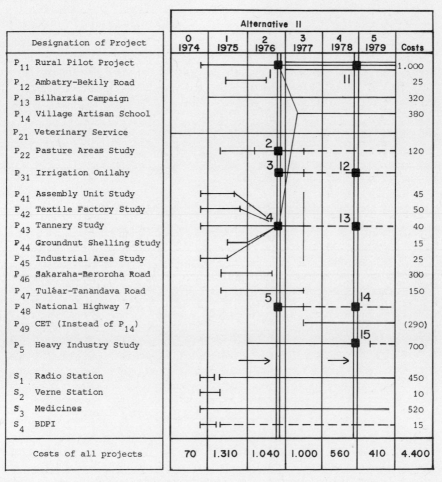

| Designation of Project | Alternative II | | | | | | Costs |
|---|---|---|---|---|---|---|---|
| | 0 1974 | 1 1975 | 2 1976 | 3 1977 | 4 1978 | 5 1979 | |
| P₁₁ Rural Pilot Project | | | | | | | 1.000 |
| P₁₂ Ambatry-Bekily Road | | | | | | | 25 |
| P₁₃ Bilharzia Campaign | | | | | | | 320 |
| P₁₄ Village Artisan School | | | | | | | 380 |
| P₂₁ Veterinary Service | | | | | | | |
| P₂₂ Pasture Areas Study | | | | | | | 120 |
| P₃₁ Irrigation Onilahy | | | | | | | |
| P₄₁ Assembly Unit Study | | | | | | | 45 |
| P₄₂ Textile Factory Study | | | | | | | 50 |
| P₄₃ Tannery Study | | | | | | | 40 |
| P₄₄ Groundnut Shelling Study | | | | | | | 15 |
| P₄₅ Industrial Area Study | | | | | | | 25 |
| P₄₆ Sakaraha-Beroroha Road | | | | | | | 300 |
| P₄₇ Tuléar-Tanandava Road | | | | | | | 150 |
| P₄₈ National Highway 7 | | | | | | | |
| P₄₉ CET (Instead of P₁₄) | | | | | | | (290) |
| P₅ Heavy Industry Study | | | | | | | 700 |
| S₁ Radio Station | | | | | | | 450 |
| S₂ Verne Station | | | | | | | 10 |
| S₃ Medicines | | | | | | | 520 |
| S₄ BDPI | | | | | | | 15 |
| Costs of all projects | 70 | 1.310 | 1.040 | 1.000 | 560 | 410 | 4.400 |

——————— Project Costs (Estimate possible)

------- Project Costs (Estimate not yet possible)

A second goal conflict affects the mining/heavy industry complex. Madagascar will need sizable amounts of new foreign private investment to exploit its coal and kaolin deposits, but this stands in contradiction to the goal of malgachization ($G_8$, $G_9$).* For technical reasons small-scale solutions, such as the extraction of coal for domestic use alone, are not possible, as large quantities of overburden have to be cleared away and expensive road networks have to be built. Only with an annual export quantity of more than about 1 million tons will the extraction of coal lead to prices that make the raw material interesting for the domestic market and for the expansion of a regional industry. Madagascar is not in a position to undertake such investments on its own in the near future. According to the regional goal system the exploitation of regional resources should have priority over the goal of malgachization, but at present there are no indications whether the political decision taken at the national level will run along these lines.

## Alternative Implementation Strategies

Two alternatives were developed that differed from each other in that a number of support projects were to be executed only after the completion of a preimplementation phase in one and right from the outset in the other (see Chart 3.1). The decision for one of the two alternatives depends on the finances available and on the political priority if the government alone is involved. In case a foreign donor comes into the picture it will be a bargaining process between the government, which most likely will have a preference for alternative II, and the foreign donor, who will want to minimize risks and will therefore prefer alternative I.

Another important flexibility component in the RDP is the incorporation of <u>decision thresholds</u>. As some projects are test projects ($P_{11}$) and others can only be secured by studies ($P_{41}$ through $P_{45}$), new findings are constantly occurring in the implementation of the RDP. As the decision on the continuation or the restructuring of individual projects have feedback effects on other projects, an evaluation of the entire RDP must be carried out at certain intervals, and decisions must be taken on the future course to be followed. In Chart 3.1 cost figures are given, should the decisions be positive. These figures include only costs that can already be estimated; in reality, therefore, the figures will be much higher after the third year. In

---

*"Malgachization" means fuller control of the Malagasy economy by Malagasy citizens.

case the decision at decision threshold I is negative, at least $2 million will have to be spent in alternative I, in contrast to $4 million in alternative II.

## IMPLEMENTATION OF THE RDP

### Institutions for Regional Development

Neglect by the central government was identified as one of the decisive factors for the underdevelopment of the South. This neglect consists not only of below-average investments but also of a below-average number of qualified professional and executive staff. As it is very difficult to get good staff to live in the province, the solution is a special regional organization, since the regular government machinery is not attractive enough. However, given the limited number of qualified executive personnel in a country like Madagascar, the decision to make a major transfer to the South would probably be just as portentous as the decision to give the South priority in investment. If the decision is not forthcoming, it is highly probable that all plans will only exist on paper.

Two new regional institutions were suggested: a planning office for the Tulear region and a regional development corporation for the urban region of Tulear and the Onilahy Valley. The main tasks of the regional planning office would be the following: (a) formulation of a development program for the entire Tulear planning region and permanent revision and updating of the program; (b) collection and compilation of regional data, permanent improvement of regional statistics, and formulation of a regional input-output table; and (c) coordination of measures taken by individual ministries, the local government, and the fokonolona. The last task is certainly the most difficult, particularly if the office is not able to exercise any pressure on the individual bodies but can only coordinate measures in various fields by exchanging information, organizing discussions with representatives of different ministries, and so on.

The first step toward a planning office as a regional branch of the Planning Ministry was already taken by sending a regional planner from UNDP. It is important that a modest staff (two assistants, stenotypists, and drivers) should be provided and continuity ensured.

As the planning office cannot execute projects itself, efficient institutions must be created for the execution of the RDP. The implementation of the integrated rural development project ($P_{11}$) could be put in the hands of a special directorate within the Ministry of Agriculture, as encouraging experience has been gained with this procedure in a similar project in the Southeast region (Sampona).

The project complex $P_2$ can provisionally be implemented by the Directorate for Animal Husbandry in the same ministry. But a regional organization should be set up for the multisectoral objectives in project complexes $P_3$ (irrigation) and $P_4$ (Tulear growth pole). A part of the irrigation area is already being managed by a regional authority with varying success. The reasons for this are partly technical (cyclone ravages and poor soils), partly due to difficulties with the population, and also due to poor management on the part of the authority. It is clear that the older regional authority will have to be incorporated in the new development corporation, as its experience must be considered, and also that success will be ensured only if the government gives the new corporation much greater priority.

The upgrading of Tulear to a growth pole calls for a package of measures that cannot be directed from the capital, Tananarive, but only from Tulear itself. These measures--e.g., development and servicing of an industrial area, formulation of an urban development plan for Tulear and its surroundings, publicity for Tulear as a location for industry, and negotiations with potential investors--cannot be executed within the framework of a traditional ministry but require the establishment of a government authority with comprehensive powers. The experience gained in Madagascar with several regional corporations should be summarized and evaluated in a study before a new institution is created; in the course of this process questions relating to the degree of autonomy, functional competence, and so on will have to be clarified.

### Participation of the Population

The regional analysis gave an indication of the antagonistic attitude of the population toward the administration. Because of this attitude a number of projects have failed in the South in the past. The best way of changing the attitude of the population is to bring about early participation in the planned projects whenever possible.

The compulsion for participation of the people also arises from the national goal system itself, where "participation" is directly mentioned ($G_{14}$, Table 3.3). Precise definitions of that term cannot be found, but it may be assumed that the concept means the collaboration in all phases of planning and implementation of those affected by the planned measures. The aim is to prevent decisions being taken without the knowledge and consent of the people, to uncover conflicts of interest between population groups as early as possible, and to find a solution that is acceptable to all. The most important forms of participation are early interviews of the affected population and the inclusion of elected representatives of the people in all subsequent phases.

Already in the preplanning phase the team made use of the opportunity to conduct a preliminary sample-type interview. In Fotadrevo, the first pilot zone for the project complex $P_1$ (integrated rural development), farmers and the fokonolona representatives were interviewed. As the time schedule for the entire survey did not permit an analysis of the social structure of the Fotadrevo fokonolona, the interview could not bring forth any statistically substantiated representation. The main objective was to test whether any fundamental resistance to project $P_1$ on the part of the population was to be expected.

The finding disclosed that not only was none to be expected, but the respondents were very interested in the introduction of ploughs combined with intensive extension, a repair workshop, and the other components of the project. Another important finding was that neither the respondents nor the fokontany representative were against foreign experts. The only condition was that the latter should not gain possession of land (this was not intended in any case).

At the regional level there is at present no people's representation in Madagascar. As expected, the political followers of the government in administration agreed with the goals of the government. It was therefore important to get the MONIMA to participate in the discussion process on regional development. Although talks with the leading representatives of that party and the party program itself showed that there was consent to regional development strategy, the MONIMA rigorously rejected the idea of foreign experts. The survey team believed, however, that, given the lack of Malagasy skilled persons, the implementation of rural development is not possible without foreign experts. In other words, there was a fundamental conflict that could jeopardize at least the agricultural part of the RDP.

In principle, the chances for participation of the population in Madagascar lie with the development of the fokonolona self-administration system. Within the frame of the RDP it was demanded that during implementation the fokonolona had to be consulted for all relevant decisions and had to be represented in all regional development corporations.

CHAPTER

# 4

**THE RURAL-DEVELOPMENT
PROJECT PROPOSED
FOR WOLLEGA, ETHIOPIA**
Christian Heimpel

This chapter is based on the findings and proposals of a field-
study group sent to Wollega Province from the German Development
Institute (GDI) at the request of the government of Ethiopia.  In the
field from November 1970 through January 1971 the study group's
mission was to determine the requirements for a regional development project RDP) in the eastern part of the province.  The term
"project" in this case refers to an ongoing activity aimed at carrying
out an ongoing development program.  Thus, the study group was
concerned both with the basic aspects of a viable rural development
program for the region and with proposing the design of the mecha-
nism for further refining and executing it.  In this case study we find
instructive descriptions of the study group's work in carrying out its
mission as well as of its "medium-package" recommendations for
the Eastern Wollega development project.

## THE PROJECT REGION

### Basic Data

The province of Wollega covers 70,000 square kilometers and
is one of the least developed areas in Ethiopia.  All but 5 percent of
the working population derive their livelihood from agriculture, but
there is very little commercial farming.  Alternative employment
opportunities hardly exist, and there is little prospect that they will
emerge in the future.  The project area, the three eastern districts
(awrajas), constitutes about one-third of the province and encom-
passes a population of about 470,000.

## Types of Farming and Land-Use Systems

Eastern Wollega has an agrarian structure based on smallholders, a system characteristic of the whole of western Ethiopia. The average farm family has 5.8 members and just over one hectare under crops. Semipermanent cultivation and unregulated ley systems predominate: The hut and crops planted around the hut for daily household requirements are permanent installations, while in the fields 3 to 6 years of cultivation alternate with 6 to 12 years of fallow.

A distinction between three major types of farming may be made in accordance with altitude and associated factors, such as soil quality and livestock numbers. High-altitude areas (above 7,700 meters) support farms growing mainly wheat, barley, and pulse. In the medium ranges (1,600 to 2,700 meters) wheat and barley are replaced by teff, maize, sorghum, and oil plants. These "maize-millet" farms may be further subcategorized into two groups: In the higher medium-range altitudes maize is part of the crop rotation, while in the poorer soils of the lower medium-range altitudes maize is excluded from the rotation system. In the latter case maize is grown in permanent fields fertilized during the dry season with pen manure, and the size of the livestock herd is therefore the limiting factor in the expansion of maize cultivation. Finally, in the hot river plains completely different conditions prevail, owing to the incidence of the tse-tse fly. Here, Nilotic migrants live on semi-nomadic forms of cultivation (maize and sorghum), using the hoe instead of the plow. Some successful large-scale farms demonstrate that this area is suitable for mechanized cultivation of maize and citrus fruit.

Generally, on the farms livestock plays a central role as a supplier of pen manure for fertilizer and draft power for the wooden plow. While population growth has led to an increase in the area under cultivation, animal fodder is not cultivated as a field crop. As a consequence, acute overgrazing has taken place.

The market integration of the farms is poor. Only coffee and red pepper are grown as cash crops in the altitudes suited for their cultivation. Apart from those only "special products," such as teff liquor, mead, local beer, gesho (Ethiopian hops), and small quantities of grain, are sold on the local markets.

The extent of diversification on the farms, even under semi-subsistence conditions, is remarkable: Up to ten sequent crops may be found in a rotation. Low farm-income levels mean that the high production risk associated with this extreme diversification carries with it the permanent threat of actual starvation. Farmers feel that their major problems are those deriving from uncontrollable forces of nature, particularly animal disease and the ravaging of crops by wildlife.

## Communications

Traffic links are poor. A single all-weather road connects the province to central Ethiopia, and it runs through only one of the three western districts. The other two districts are connected to this main artery by feeder roads that are not passable in the rainy season. Other roads that may be indicated on maps of the region were built during the Italian occupation and are no longer serviceable. Agricultural products are transported as headloads or on donkeys, with the exception of some road transport on the roads mentioned. Bullock carts are unknown.

## Land Ownership and Tenancy

Next to rural administration, the greatest problem of the region is the agrarian structure, which, as throughout Ethiopia, may be characterized as tenancy in the form of share cropping. In eastern Wollega a survey of 188 farms revealed the following land-ownership pattern:

| | |
|---|---|
| Landowners | 31.4% |
| Tenants with additional land of their own | 18.6% |
| Tenants | 50.0% |
| Tenants paying fixed rents (mostly in kind) | 35.2% |
| Sharecroppers in paying 20 to 25% | 40.6% |
| Sharecroppers in paying 33-1/3% | 5.2% |
| Sharecroppers in paying 50% | 19.0% |

The tenancy contracts are generally concluded orally. The consequent uncertainty of the length of tenancy may stand in the way of long-term investments in the tenant's farm.

## Local Administration: The Balabat System

The Balabats are members of reputed families who, when Wollega was conquered by the Amharas more than 100 years ago, were permitted to keep their land (Siso land) and, as a reward for loyalty to their new rulers, were awarded powerful and important positions, a limited right to arbitrate in legal matters, and the right to collect taxes. The system continues to this day, and the Balabats therefore form a kind of lower rural aristocracy, as well as the lowest level of official rural administration. Land purchased later combined with the Siso land commonly makes them prosperous

landowners. In their areas they are responsible for law and order,
and some maintain their own prisons.

The dual function of the Balabats as representatives of the traditional rural society and the lowest officials of the executive constitutes a problem for rural development. The economic mobilization
of the rural population and increased social mobility would bring
about a relative deterioration in the social and economic position of
the Balabats, who, through the power deriving from their official
capacities, can slow down the pace of development considerably.

## Regional Administration

In Ethiopia rural administration is characterized by the juxta-
position of two administrative structures: the regional administration under the governor of the province at the level of awrajas,
woredas (subdistricts) and the Balabat areas; and the provincial offices of the central ministries. The governor of the province is responsible for the coordination of the ministerial offices and the di-
rectives issued to them, but in technical matters the offices are
supervised by the central ministry concerned. Within the ministerial
provincial offices a further distinction may be made between the
"traditional" ministries, such as Interior, Law, and Finance, and
the "development" ministries, such as Agriculture, Community Development, and Land Reform.

Provincial offices of the traditional ministries have an extremely strong influence on the other provincial offices and the regional administrative bodies at the district and subdistrict level,
because they govern finances, personnel policy, and legal jurisdic-
tion, whereas the other provincial offices have virtually no supporting
administrative structure apart from a few clerks and a small number
of village-level workers. The strongest positions in the administration are occupied by the law-and-order-oriented provincial offices of
the central ministries and the status-quo-oriented regional and local
administration.

## THE WORK OF THE PROJECT STUDY GROUP

### Study-Group Approach

The "region" under consideration by the study group, the three
eastern districts of Wollega Province, was predelineated by administrative boundaries. Thus, "regional planning" in this case meant
the planning of measures for the promotion of the rural economy for

a region arbitrarily defined, from an economic point of view.  The
low level of sectoral integration in Wollega dictated that the delineation of a "region" in terms of a functional system could be meaningfully undertaken only at a later stage.  Also, since other natural resources outside the agricultural sector were not known, the RDP
being designed could not aim at a simultaneous promotion of various
economic sectors and at the establishment of a growth pole.  Rather,
it was decided that economic development, primarily agricultural
development, would be fostered wherever concrete starting points
could be found.

## Formal Tasks of the Study Group

The study group's ultimate mission, the preparation of an RDP
proposal, called for the carrying out of four principal tasks within a
three-month period:  empirical analysis, identification of the main
components of the program to be proposed, planning for these elements of the program, and designing implementation machinery.

On its arrival in the field the study group was confronted not
only with the usual lack of data but also with contradictory information and, as later became clear, with false information.  Nothing was
on record concerning farm organization, agrarian structure, location
of agricultural products, or other data of the most basic kind.  The
empirical analysis that had to be undertaken went considerably beyond the collection of statistical data, for data alone, to the extent
they could be obtained or generated, would never provide the sort of
grasp of the existing situation necessary for the planning of a meaningful development program.  This "grasp" or "feel" for the existing
situation and its antecedents involves a familiarity with the intrinsic
laws governing the rural economy of a region, and as it emerges, a
checklist implicitly or explicitly emerges along with it, by which the
many ideas constantly being produced for the makeup of the program
can be gauged.

Program "ideas" (components and elements) were sought from
six sources:

1. those already submitted before the study group arrived;
2. information on markets for agricultural products, the production
   potential of the region, and the available technologies for producing marketable output from the region's resources;
3. information on the felt needs of the future beneficiaries of the
   project--i.e., identification of project goals in terms of "problem solutions as desired by the farmers";

4. information on the development strategy of the country, within
   which the project to be proposed would have to be integrated;
5. comparative analysis of farm types--i.e., the observed devia-
   tions in levels of development among the subregions of eastern
   Wollega;
6. the experiences of other countries and projects.

From these sources the study group culled a set of development program proposals through a process of continuing internal discussions
aimed at isolating those that seemed workable within the project
context. Those then were subjected to calculations with a view to
their economic implications and were discussed with officials, poli-
ticians, and other experts toward a fuller assessment of their practicability within the context of existing social and political reality.

The planning of the actual development program elements, including time phasing, and subregional allocations was, of course,
the core of the study group's work. However, this was carried out in
more or less traditional manner and need not be discussed in detail
here.

The fourth, and in many ways the most complex and delicate,
formal task for the study group was the design of the implementation
machinery for the development program. This had to include the
proposed project's administrative structure, its integration with the
agricultural administration of Ethiopia, and its link-up with foreign
aid administration, in connection with existing and potential future
foreign-aid projects in the area. It was clear that such a task could
not be accomplished by producing desk models or "organigrammes"
or whatnot. On the contrary, this sometimes touchy political issue
can only be resolved with the help of political means, that is, by obtaining a consensus through constant discussion and revision.


### Study Group Work Methods

It was immediately clear that there was no useful application
for aggregated quantitative or mathematical planning tools. Even
for the most theoretically simple techniques of this type both the
basic data required and the argument of relevance were lacking. The
low degree of intersectoral dependence did not permit the identification of linkages, flows, and other standard features of regional and
interregional models.

Moreover, a uniform, formalized, quantitative method for
identifying the principal contours of a development program does not
exist. And this lack is understandable, for a process in which

creativity and consensus play--or should play--such important roles cannot possibly be abstracted and formalized. However, within the framework of a logically structured approach numerous formalized methodological tools can be creatively applied. These range from techniques of microsocial and microeconomic field surveys to market analyses and cost-and-time studies. The essential point that must be borne in mind with regard to these techniques is that they perform service functions--that is, their selection and use must be dictated by the conditions and objectives of the study, and not the other way around. Since the overall shape and constituent parts of the development program only emerge clearly in the course of field work, the very selection of the most appropriate techniques becomes a planning problem that can only be solved in the field. If the study group would have come to the field and attempted to operate within the rigid framework of a predesigned methodological approach, the range of possible project proposals would have been seriously and unrealistically circumscribed. In effect, the signals would have been set at a time when no one knew in which direction the train was going to move.

During the field survey in eastern Wollega a number of empirical and calculatory methods were applied. Much importance was attached to thorough empirical survey work, not only because reliable basic data on the region were unavailable but also because the program proposals made to the study group by the ministries in Addis Ababa had no empirical base at all. The empirical work was undertaken in three principal areas: microeconomic surveys in agriculture, market analysis, and administration. With regard to microeconomic surveys in agriculture, an attempt was first made to gain a general picture of land-use systems in the region and then to examine the internal organization of individual farm types, in order to obtain an information base to enable the estimation of the probable impacts on the farms of various possible measures. Thus, by means of the farm-budgeting method, the effects of introducing certain "existing" innovations, such as the application of fertilizers, on the organization of the farm and the income of the farmer were investigated. Also, the question of whether some of these innovations could be seriously considered at all, given the existing constraints, could be examined. At the same time, a survey was undertaken in a crucial area: land-ownership and tenancy patterns.

In the surveys the study group applied the usual methods of empirical field research. Fortunately, the research was undertaken during the harvest period, so that it was possible to measure physically the area unit yields of the most important crops and to have a direct means of evaluating farm performance.

Contrary to expectation, the practical difficulties in field work did not arise with regard to farmer interviews or the measurement of fields, but rather in the selection of the survey sample. It was impossible to cover all the farms, and difficulty was encountered persuading local officials that the study group was not mainly interested in visiting the "best" farmers, often the Balabats themselves.

The detailed market analysis ran parallel to the farm surveys and was designed not only to enable a forecast of markets for the most important crops but also to serve as a "feeler" for the farm surveys. Thus, if a certain crop appeared at specific local markets, more questions regarding this crop were asked in the course of the farm surveys.

The market analysis presented the greatest methodological difficulties, owing to the nature of the work. As expected, it was often impossible to get information on prices and turnover from the local dealers. The role of the landowners also remained ambiguous. There were reasons to assume that the landowners sold in kind a considerable part of the commodities they received or even that the marketed surplus of agriculture was often identical with the crop-share of the landowners, but for obvious reasons this flow of goods could not be documented or evaluated in monetary terms. So, in addition to a survey of local markets through test purchases (which should have been carried out over a longer period of time in order to get more information on the important question of price fluctuations), an investigation of marketing conditions in the capital city, where data were more readily available, was carried out.

The third area of empirical work involved a survey of agricultural administration and associated modern and traditional rural institutions. First, diagrams were drawn up on the basis of the organization charts of the various administrative units in order to obtain a static picture of the decision and information flows in the overall administrative system. Then, on the basis of the competencies and functions of these institutions, an attempt was made to follow the flow of some project-relevant decisions (e.g., the allocation of funds) in the system, thereby to obtain some insights into the administrative bottlenecks of project implementation. Finally, alternatives to eliminate the bottlenecks through a partial modification of the institutional structure were discussed, first within the study group, and then with the Ethiopian administration.

Taking the microeconomic analysis of smallholders as the point of departure, the necessary services (extension, credit, and so on) and the overhead investments (e.g., infrastructure and general project costs) were computed by the usual methods of calculation. The cost estimates together with the projection for monetary income increase of the farms were compiled in a cost-benefit analysis that, however, was deliberately reduced to a simplified form.

A network system was used for the time schedule of the program. However, its main purpose was not the usual function of time reduction but rather the clarification of the logical linkages of project activities and project decisions in the time sequence.

The field surveys were performed over a period of about six weeks, during which three team members covered the farms, one covered the market, and one covered administration. The rest of the study group's time was spent in Addis Ababa evaluating the field surveys, conducting test calculations on potential measures to be proposed, and drafting a preliminary report. Throughout the study the team worked as a single unit, making no distinctions between "data collectors," "producers of ideas," and "writers." The Ethiopian Ministry of Agriculture had placed a room in the ministry at the disposal of the study group, and this made it possible to include Ethiopian officials in the discussion of the project at all stages.

Great significance was attached to the planning of implementation machinery in preparation of the project proposal. Implementation problems were tackled in the following manner. First, in the belief that the probability of ultimate implementation is greatest when interest in implementation is strong and widespread, an attempt was made to bring out a consensus concerning the goals of the project to be proposed. This consensus had to be arrived at among the rural population (the beneficiary group) on the one hand, and the political decision makers in Ethiopian and foreign-aid administration on the other. Where this was not possible, an attempt was made at least to take into account the perceived interests of all concerned. Second, care was taken to build sufficient flexibility into the project design so as to prevent a collision between an excessively tight and detailed proposal on one side and, on the other, facts and events that the study group may have overlooked, estimated or interpreted wrongly, or that were simply unpredictable. A series of options were left open, sufficient to enable adequate room for maneuver during negotiations on the ultimate form of the project. Finally, the project concept proposed incorporated the implementation machinery and its integration into the Ethiopian administrative setup. That is, the mechanisms for carrying out the development program were made an integral part of the project design.


## Presentation of Study Group Recommendations

The study group understood that its report would be in the nature of a preliminary document and that the final decisions on the project would be taken by Ethiopian officials after internal discussions in which members of the study group would not participate.

Therefore, when drafting the report, due consideration was given to
the fact that it would serve as a basis for a political bargaining process. The central task of the report was seen as clearly spelling out
the essentials of the project proposal in a convincing manner, rather
than the provision of copious quantitative detail. While the basic
data can change somewhat, it was felt that the fundamental terms of
reference of such a project must have a fixity of purpose. The formulation of the basic principles underlying the project proposal
therefore made up a separate and central part of the report.

Following the drafting of the report, proposals concerning
specific project components were presented, along with the implementation activities and associated data on subsectoral, subregional,
and time allocations.

Finally, the results of the field work and other research were
provided in a straightforward compendium format. Those data not
directly needed for support of the project proposal were compiled in
a report annex so that they would be available to the project staff for
use in its practical work.

## BASIC PRINCIPLES OF THE PROPOSED PROJECT

In keeping with the agricultural policy principles of the Ethiopian Master Plan, the study group took the basic objective of the
RDP to be the quickest and most widespread introduction of measures
to raise incomes and standards of living. The "operationalized project goal," therefore, was to introduce a useful package of simple
innovations and the measures necessary to sustain them, in a way
that would maximize the population of the region favorably affected.

### Medium-Package Project

The study group felt that the project would not proceed beyond
a short-lived initial success if production-increasing innovations
were introduced without attaching greater weight than previously to
the promotion of supporting measures. This feeling arose not only
from awareness of the generally recognized interdependence of all
social factors in rural areas but also from observation of concrete
examples in the case of Wollega. For example, the benefits of a
"minimum-package" measure (the introduction of fertilizers for
certain crops) had been offset in certain instances by a decline in
work capacity resulting from malaria.

Furthermore, minimum-package or localized limited innovations did not hold the promise of resulting in a self-sustaining

long-run improvement trend.   The farmers in Wollega had attained
an extremely high standard of subsistence economy by means of trial
and error.   It was true that farm income could be increased in the
short-run without changing the present farm system, merely by introducing some short-term measures fairly certain of success, such
as commercial fertilizers and improved seed, and these could be
absorbed most efficiently by the farmers through trial and error.
But soon the point would be reached where more complex measures
would be required if gains were to be sustained and pushed farther.
Measures, such as marketing policy, supervised credits, transition
to field fodder cultivation, new rotations, and cash crops, among
others, require knowledge and a budget that go well beyond those involved in trial-and-error methods.

     Indeed, the problem of the Ethiopian government with regard to
general agricultural improvement was similar to that of its farmers.
The Wollega project was therefore viewed as a necessary supplement
to Ethiopian agricultural policy:  Just as it would seek to provide support measures for innovations introduced in the region, the project
would itself be a support measure for all Ethiopian agriculture.   The
proposed program was intended as a "spearhead" and demonstration
project for the introduction of far-reaching innovations throughout
the country.

     To accomplish these ends, the proposed measures would have
to be regionally dispersed and have a broad approach, covering many
related subsectors.  In particular, credit, promotion of input-supply
production, improved marketing, and improved tenancy patterns
would always have to be introduced as a "package," even in the
short run.  For the longer run, measures were required in the areas
of research (in order to refine existing and produce additional innovations), health, and infrastructure.  Since the proposed project encompassed the principles of packages of interrelated measures on
the one hand, and regional distribution on the other, it lay between
the two extremes of comprehensive and minimum-package approaches:
it was therefore dubbed a "medium-package project."


### Orientation to Felt Needs


     Frank talks with farmers during the farm surveys revealed
that their major felt needs were for wildlife control and the eradica-
tion of animal diseases.  Measures addressing these problems were
incorporated into the project proposal.  Great importance was attached to this, since implementation of a project, especially one
oriented to the participation of the rural population, depends greatly
upon the degree of its responsiveness to their direct needs.  Officials

of the central administration tend to live in a world apart from the rural poor, and to a significant extent a maintenance of their positions of status is associated with a maintenance of spiritual distance from the rural community. Authorities in the central city may not relate with seriousness to problems of major import to the rural poor, such as the control of maize-field-devastating baboon herds. It was clear that if such problems would not receive major attention in the project, the development program would not be taken seriously by the rural community (a situation that had, in fact, occurred in the past).

## Ongoing Intraproject Planning

The planning of an agricultural project of the sort under discussion always involves an ongoing process of revision. This particularly applies to a project that is necessarily burdened with uncertainty regarding technical, economic, and social factors and, in addition, is oriented toward steady spatial and sectoral expansion.

This type of permanent program planning cannot be undertaken from outside. The most an unbiased outsider can do, apart from setting the general line to be followed, is give help in the field of methods and evaluate the planning process as such. But he lacks the necessary insider information for the detailed planning of measures, the selection of the region, and the like.

Intraproject planning is based on the principle of small circuits. The information continuously obtained in the course of project implementation is used directly for plan revision or the formulation of short-term subplans. The management of the proposed Wollega project, composed of both Ethiopians and foreign aid personnel, was given the responsibility for this and was charged with drawing up annual plans for approval by the appropriate representatives of the Ethiopian government. The proposed ongoing intraproject planning process also included preparation of the necessary technical studies. While outside expert help might be sought for these, implementation was the exclusive responsibility of the permanent staff to be set up for the project.

In order to facilitate effective intraproject planning, it was proposed that the project management be given a measure of decision-making power with regard to the use of project funds. While such power would obviously have to be seriously circumscribed (it could not be permitted to overstep the limits of the current annual budget, for example), it would have to be great enough to provide not only the feeling but also the fact of a capability to respond to circumstances in a manner consistent with the overall objectives of the project.

## The Expansion System

The project was fundamentally oriented toward a broad involvement of the rural population.  However, owing to limited resources
on the one hand and to lack of information on the actual impact of
development measures on the other, it seemed wisest to begin operations on a modest scale in dispersed areas of the region.

Thus, the necessity arose to outline the machinery for the
gradual expansion of the project.  This expansion path followed the
"point-line-network" system.* According to this approach, innovations are first tested for feasibility at one "point" and then modified
if necessary.  In the next phase this innovation is introduced along a
"line" in different locations--i.e., under different environmental
conditions--in order to identify the necessary regional or local modifications.  Once this phase has been completed, the innovation can
be spread like a "network" over the whole subregion as soon as possible.  A "point" in this approach is always a subregional unit--e.g.,
a group of farms that operate under similar locational conditions.
Within the framework of the proposed Wollega project these starting
points were identical with the subcenters, which, under the guidance
of the central project administration in the provincial capital, were
to introduce the primary innovations in agriculture.

Because of the size of the project region it was proposed that
a start should be made simultaneously from several "points."  The
expansion proceeded in two dimensions, therefore:  First, each
subregional starting point of the project moved through the above-
mentioned phases, and, second, the number of these starting points
was to be increased until the entire region would be covered in the
network phase.

The study group limited its proposal to the establishment of
the first three subcenters, one in each of the three eastern districts
of Wollega.  The anticipated participation per subcenter could be
calculated from the capacity of the project staff (extension agents),
the duration of the "point" and "line" phases, and the number of
subcenters.

## Research

The research principle had two basic aspects.  One was that
the proposed innovations and accompanying packages of measures be

---

*On this, see, E. M. Kulp, Rural Development Planning (New
York: Praeger, 1970), p. 56.

tested in selected farms and finally adopted only after their application proved out in practice, as originally proposed or in modified form. This applied in particular to the level of innovations and accompanying packages that implied a basic transformation in types of farming. A typical example involved the promotion of animal husbandry, success in which depended not only on the technical coefficients and economic data that could be obtained from experimental tests but also on the ability of agricultural policy to control the process. There, the function of the program was to assume the economic risk by financing part of the costs arising for the farmer-- e.g., investment in a fodder silo--in the testing and introductory phase from the research budget of the program.

The other was that the project as a whole was to be seen, in a sense, as an ongoing research project. In particular, it was thought that useful information and experience would be gained from the administrative structure of the project as proposed by the study group, and as well from the study of impacts of the socioagricultural measures introduced. From this point of view the project had the function of an antenna in the trial-and-error process of formulating overall national agricultural policy.

## Reduction of Foreign Input

Steps had to be taken from the very start to prevent the project from following the pattern of other foreign aid projects and swelling into one of those regional superprojects that are so very problematic for both the donor and the recipient. Moreover, provision had to be made to terminate the project at short notice without visiting hardship on the recipient in the event that insurmountable difficulties, such as in domestic or foreign policy, arose.

The gradual expansion outlined in the project design obviously could not be made dependent upon a corresponding increase in foreign aid. On the other hand, it was obvious that existing personnel conditions would not permit the subcenters to be staffed by Ethiopians alone. It was therefore proposed that the first three subcenters should be staffed with foreign experts as directors but that new subcenters--i.e., new point-line-network units--should be established only after the existing subcenters had entered the network phase and could be handed over to an Ethiopian expert. This would ensure that long-term progress of the project would not depend on an increase of foreign aid, and that the development aid component in the overall project could in fact be reduced steadily.

## Institution Building

Three major problems had to be confronted with regard to the administrative structure of the proposed project. First, a compromise had to be found between the need for an independent project administration and the need for participation of all major bodies in Ethiopia's central and regional administration. Second, it was necessary to prevent the foreign experts initially involved from gaining an unduly strong position in the project administration, while it was evident that, owing to the lack of trained Ethiopian personnel, a number of key administrative positions would have to be filled for some time by foreigners. Third, it was essential that the rural population be integrated into the decision-making process of the project.

The study group first proposed that the program should not be integrated into the provincial administration of Wollega but rather that an independent administrative unit be created within the Ministry of Agriculture. The other technical ministries concerned and the provincial government would be coordinated in an administrative "advisory council" that would have to approve the annual plans of operation submitted by the project management. The emphasis placed on the Ministry of Agriculture had the purpose of strengthening the position of the "development-oriented" parts of the central administration vis-a-vis the provincial administration.

The second proposal was that the project administration should at the same time become the regional representative of the Ministry of Agriculture in the whole of Wollega. The Ethiopian director of the development program would also serve as the Wollega Provincial Officer of the Ministry of Agriculture. This arrangement would prevent the parallel existence of a strong project administration and a weak local agricultural administration.

A great deal of caution had to be exercised in the proposals concerning farmer organizations. Thus, the empty phrase "cooperative," so popular in many reports on planning, was avoided, and joint action by the farmers was envisaged in only one field in which the farmers themselves felt it was necessary, namely, tax collection. In order to eliminate the customary bribery and fraud in tax collection, and in order to ensure that farmers did not have to pay taxes just when producers' prices were at their lowest, it was suggested that "tax-paying units" be established. These units would encompass those farmers living within the area of influence of the subcenter, who would select an agent to pay their collective taxes to the responsible authority and collect the receipts. Through this agent the project could grant the farmers a tax-payment credit, to be repaid together with other input credits. Thus, the project could intervene in the tax-paying process to the benefit of the farmers without becoming directly involved in tax-collection-related activities.

CHART 4.1

The Three Phases of Institution–Building Proposed for the Wollega Project

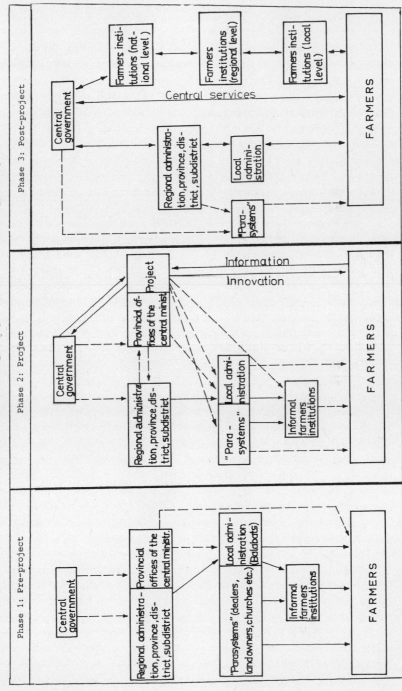

Apart from these proposals for overcoming specific problems, it was essential that the project design incorporate a prestructuring of the long-term process of rural institution building and spell out the role the project would play in this process. On the one hand, it was necessary to make the administration of the project resistant to pressures that might be exerted by the tradition-oriented institutions, including the status-quo-oriented sections of the central and regional administrations. On the other hand, comprehensive subsectoral and regional projects with a strong administrative position of their own run the danger of falling into a form of social isolation that can not only stand in the way of promoting social spread effects but can also become a threat to the very existence of the project in certain situations.

Required was a procedure whereby the "administrative protection" necessary at the beginning of the project would be gradually relaxed; an increasing number of functions would be redelegated back to the "parasystems" and the general government administration; and ultimately a situation would develop in which a separate project administration would be superfluous, and information and innovations would flow through a general system of agropolitical institutions. But such a redelegation can only work if the institutions concerned are integrated into the control system of the project administration. For example, rural dealers can be integrated into the marketing system of the project only if they accept certain conditions imposed by the government, such as with regard to the quality of their products.

Chart 4.1 shows the three most important phases of the process of institutional change as proposed for the Wollega project. The preproject situation was described briefly earlier. Since the Balabats are generally landowners or rural dealers themselves, the parasystem and the local administration form a united block of status-quo-oriented decision makers. Under the circumstances there was no way of avoiding the establishment of a separate project administration to ensure a direct line of contact between farmers and the decision-making system of the central government (Phase 2). At the same time, by assuming the functions of the parasystems (credit, marketing, and social services), it would attempt to weaken the bonds of dependency of the farmers on these institutions. Furthermore, the provincial offices of the central government directly relevant to the project would be closely attached to the project, and ties between these and the traditional provincial administration would be weakened. In the third phase information and innovations are shown as passing through the channels of a reorganized regional administration, a system of farmer organizations, and some central agencies. In this final phase projects in the traditional sense of the term no longer exist.

# 5

## SOCIOECONOMIC ANALYSIS AND IDENTIFICATION OF A PRIORITY PROJECT IN THE KOSI REGION, NEPAL

Dieter Weiss

This chapter summarizes the experience and findings of a field mission of the German Development Institute (GDI) in cooperation with the Centre of Economic Development and Administration, Kathmandu, to the Kosi Zone in Eastern Nepal from November 1971 to February 1972.[1] The terms of reference were to prepare a report for the Nepalese Planning Commission containing an analysis of the regional socioeconomic structure and the identification of the most urgent development needs of the region. Within this process the team tried to test the organization, timing, and methods of a reduced planning approach subject to constraints of manpower and time. In particular the following questions were of interest:

1. How long should a first overview of the situation last?
2. How should the first problem identification in the field at the beginning of the empirical analysis be organized?
3. How should the information flow and the discussion process within the team be organized?
4. How long should the subsequent phase of detailed analysis of objectives and of the development potential in the individual sectors and subregions last?
5. At which point should the preliminary surveys of the sectors, subregions, major problems, and projects be brought to an end, and when should a decision on the direction and the (sectoral and subregional) concentration of the further search process for operational project proposals be taken?
6. At what time should the results be discussed with the decision makers? i.e., when should the feedback from the development potential to the goal level occur?

7. How much time should be reserved for the detailed formulation of the project and program proposals?

8. How much time should be left for the final discussion with the decision makers and for reformulations or modifications of the proposed project and program alternatives?

9. Should another limited field survey be conducted if the decision makers require additional detailed information on the basis of the newly gained insights into the actual problems?

The team consisted of the team leader, his Nepalese counterpart, and six young German professionals. During the empirical field surveys five Nepalese assistants (students from the colleges in Biratnagar and Dharan in the survey region) joined the team and also served as interpreters for the interviews in the region.

## STRUCTURE OF THE REGION

Kosi Zone covers an area extending about 110 kilometers from north to south and about 35 kilometers from east to west (see Map 5.1). It consists of three main geographical belts: the Himalayan chain of 8,000-meter mountains in the north; south of that chain, the Hills with altitudes up to 3,500 meters; in the south the flat Terai, an extension of the great Indian plain. Biratnagar in the Terai on the Indian border is the largest industrial town in Nepal with 11,000 employed persons, of whom 5,200 work in the jute industry; 1,600 in the rice and oil mills; and the rest in sugar factories, food and fruit processing, wood and furniture industries, manufacture of bricks and tiles, and the metal-working and textile industries. The total industrial output per annum amounts to about Rs 200 million (approximately $20 million). The Terai is very strongly oriented toward India; a large number of the bigger traders are Indians with their headquarters in Calcutta. Dharan is a trade center at the foot of the Hills. Dhankuta, Terhathum, and Chainpur are small towns with 3,000 to 6,500 inhabitants each and function as communication and trade centers for the Hills. Detailed information on the region is hardly available. The total population is put at 400,000 in the Terai and 350,000 in the Hills of the Kosi Zone. Per capita income is about Rs 300 ($30) in the Hills and about Rs 900 ($90) in the Terai.

## IDENTIFICATION OF OBJECTIVES

Before departure to the field an attempt was made to uncover the development objectives that could be relevant for regional planning in the Kosi Zone from various plan documents and other available material. The result was the following vague, multidimensional, and partly conflicting catalogue: increase of regional income; lowering of the income disparity between the Hills and the Terai; better utilization of local resources; strengthening the economic integration of the Terai and the Hills; increase of regional employment; increase of exports (at present, mainly raw and processed jute); provision of social services, particularly in the remote areas; control of migration from the Hills to the Terai; planned settlement of migrants from the Hills in the Terai; stronger national integration of different ethnic groups.

On the regional level there were grounds to assume that the population of the Terai, which is mainly occupied in agriculture, was primarily interested in raising agricultural yields through better access to irrigation and fertilizers. It was not possible to identify the economic and social situation in the Hills before departure. Two hypotheses were formulated by the team: First, the Hill population is primarily interested in raising its basic food and income level through promotion of agriculture and possibly handicrafts, and through transport facilities; second, the major reason for migration is the nonavailability of social services, such as schools, medical care, drinking water, and so on.

MAP 5.1

Location of Kosi Zone

## FORMULATION OF PRELIMINARY PROJECT
## AND PROGRAM HYPOTHESES

Against the background of those considerations the team drew up four project and program hypotheses.

The first concerned a transportation project for Dharan and Dhankuta. Dhankuta lies one day's trekking distance north of Dharan. A Dharan-Dhankuta road project will be of the utmost importance for the economic and social north-south integration of the zone and the Hills in the eastern and western neighboring zones.

The second concerned an industrial program for Biratnagar. According to the information available, several branches of industry in Biratnagar appeared to be having increasing difficulties in selling their products in Nepal and in exporting them (mainly to India). This probably applied largely to industries facing growing competition from synthetic products--e.g., the jute industry. Industry will evidently have a considerable effect on the regional economy in the future, particularly on the opportunities for marketing agricultural raw materials. The team envisaged an analysis of the forward and backward linkages of selected industrial branches and an empirical survey of consumer budgets in order to identify the present purchasing power and the consumer habits of the population and to estimate the future demand for various industrial products in the region.

The third hypothesis concerned a dam project in the Terai. The Kankai dam project, already being discussed, is located in the neighboring Mechi Zone, but it could have considerable spread effects on the Terai districts of the Kosi Zone, particularly with respect to irrigation and power supply for agriculture and industry.

The fourth concerned a small-scale development program for the Hill population. A promotion program in agriculture, handicrafts, and social services was envisaged. Since most of Nepal consists of hilly areas, economic and social development cannot ignore the necessity of development efforts for these areas. But apparently the problem that arises here is that higher economic growth rates are probably obtained if investment is carried out in the Terai. The locational disadvantages of the remote northern regions are obvious (transportation costs, availability of transportation facilities, availability of raw material and skilled labor, access to markets, economies of scale, and so on). Three strategies for the development of the Hills were considered:

1. A development program based on subsidies for economically inefficient activities. This approach was followed in India in the course of the campaign for small-scale industries in the first few years after independence, and it failed. Nepal will probably not even be in a position to finance such a course of action.

2.  Promotion of economically competitive products for which a market exists.  In view of the disadvantages of the Hills with respect to production and transportation costs, it is probably expedient to promote only those products that are different from competing products in the Terai or in India (e.g., citrus fruit, certain vegetables, seed potatoes, perhaps tea and animal products), products that can exploit the special climatic advantages of the Hills.

3.  The improvement of social services, such as schools, medical care, drinking water, housing, and so on, to the Hill population.  This approach was eventually linked to the first two.  The team was uncertain how such large-scale provision of social services would influence migration.  Virtually no information was available on the economic and social structure of the Hills.

## METHOD APPROACH AND SCHEDULING

### Method Approach

A regional input-output table was selected as the methodological frame for the analysis of the region's socioeconomic structure (see Table 5.1).  Such a table had not previously been drawn up for either the individual zones or Nepal as a whole.  The team was aware that the construction of an input-output table would involve a considerable amount of effort.  Despite this, the input-output approach was chosen because it offers a clear logical structure for regional analysis and for the evaluation of the regional-spread effects of projects and programs that is apparently superior to the secondary-benefit approach of cost-benefit analysis.  The construction of the table seemed to be a feasible proposition because one could reasonably assume that the intersectoral interdependence between the individual sectors (and, consequently, the body of data required) would not be too great.  The important element appeared to be the inclusion of the interregional aspects through three export columns and three import rows for the rest of Nepal, India, and the rest of the world. (On the construction of an interregional input-output table, see Chapter 7.)

### Transportation Project

For the analysis of the transportation project various transport models were examined for their possible applicability.  The model by Bos and Koyck was discussed in detail as a logical basic structure for the anticipated problems.[2]

TABLE 5.1

Input-Output Table of the Kosi Zone, 1969-70
(in Rs thousand)*

| Output | Intermediate Demand | | | | | | | | | |
|---|---|---|---|---|---|---|---|---|---|---|
| | Hill Economy Without Services | | | | | | | | | |
| Input | 1. | 2. | 3. | 4. | 5. | 6. | 7. | 8. | 9. | 10. |
| **Intermediate Inputs** | | | | | | | | | | |
| Hill economy without services | | | | | | | | | | |
| 1. Paddy | 560 | | | | | | ... | | | |
| 2. Millet | | 66 | | | | | ... | | | |
| 3. Maize | | | 560 | | | | ... | | | |
| 4. Potatoes | | | | 1,570 | | | | | | |
| 5. Citrus fruits | | | | | | | | | | |
| 6. Medicinal herbs | | | | | | | | | | |
| 7. Livestock | 2,180 | | 5,100 | 375 | | | | 1,062 | | |
| 8. Other agricultural products | | | | | | | ... | 288 | 31 | |
| 9. Brass utensils | | | | | | | | | | |
| 10. Other products | | | | | | | | | | |
| Σ     1-10 | 2,740 | 66 | 5,660 | 1,945 | – | – | ... | 1,350 | 31 | – |
| Terai agriculture | | | | | | | | | | |
| 11. Paddy | | | | | | | | | | |
| 12. Wheat | | | | | | | | | | |
| 13. Oil seeds | | | | | | | | | | |
| 14. Jute | | | | | | | | | | |
| 15. Sugarcane | | | | | | | | | | |
| 16. Livestock | | | | | | | | | | |
| 17. Forestry | | | | | | | | | | |
| 18. Other agricultural products | | | | | | | | | | |
| Σ     11-18 | – | – | – | – | – | – | – | – | – | – |
| Terai industry | | | | | | | | | | |
| 19. Jute processing | | | | | | | | | | |
| 20. Rice and oil | | | | | | | | | | |
| 21. Sugar refineries | | | | | | | | | | |
| 22. Fruit and food processing | | | | | | | | | | |
| 23. Other industries | | | | | | | | | | |
| Σ     19-23 | – | – | – | – | – | – | – | – | – | – |
| 24. Services | 385 | – | 960 | 305 | – | – | – | 12 | 98 | – |
| 1-24 | 3,125 | 66 | 6,620 | 2,250 | – | – | ... | 1,362 | 129 | – |
| **Primary Inputs** | | | | | | | | | | |
| 25. Import: rest of Nepal | | | | | | | | | | |
| 26. Import: India | | | | | | | | | | |
| 27. Import: wages, India | | | | | | | | | | |
| 28. Import: rest of world | | | | | | | | | | |
| 29. Others | 17,225 | 4,374 | 24,400 | 6,310 | 1,120 | 1,550 | 9,367 | 1,505 | 252 | 1,230 |
| Σ     25-29 | 17,225 | 4,374 | 24,400 | 6,310 | 1,120 | 1,550 | 9,367 | 1,505 | 571 | 1,230 |
| Total inputs   Σ 1-29 | 20,350 | 4,440 | 31,020 | 8,560 | 1,120 | 1,550 | 9,367 | 2,867 | 700 | 1,230 |

Note: Ellipses indicate that flows exist, but data not available; dashes indicate nil or negligible.

*Rs 10 equals about $1.

| | | | | | Intermediate Demand | | | | | | | | | |
| Terai Agriculture | | | | | | | | Terai Industry | | | | | | Σ 1-24 |
| 11. | 12. | 13. | 14. | 15. | 16. | 17. | 18. | 19. | 20. | 21. | 22. | 23. | 24. | |
|---|---|---|---|---|---|---|---|---|---|---|---|---|---|---|
| | | | | | | | | | | | | | | 560 |
| | | | | | | | | | | | | | | 66 |
| | | | | | | | | | | | | | | 560 |
| | | | | | | | 273 | | | | | | | 1,843 |
| | | | | | | | | | | | 40 | | | 40 |
| | | | | | | | | | | | | | | - |
| | | | | | | | | | | | | | | 8,717 |
| | | | | | | | | | | | | | | 319 |
| | | | | | | | | | | | | | | - |
| | | | | | | | | | | | | | | - |
| - | - | - | - | - | - | - | 273 | - | - | - | 40 | - | - | 12,105 |
| 7,605 | | | ... | | | | | | 90,930 | | | | | 98,535 |
| | 534 | | ... | | | | | | | | | | | 534 |
| | | 532 | | | | | | | 3,860 | | | | | 4,392 |
| | | | 705 | | | | | 27,800 | | | | | | 28,505 |
| | | | | 565 | | | | | | 3,920 | | | | 4,483 |
| 44,640 | 2,400 | 927 | 12,000 | 430 | | | 1,501 | | | | 60 | | | 61,958 |
| | | | | | ... | | | | | | 80 | 1,828 | 20 | 1,928 |
| | | | | | | | 828 | | | | | 2,390 | | 3,218 |
| 52,245 | 2,934 | 1,459 | 12,705 | 995 | ... | - | 2,329 | 27,800 | 94,790 | 4,000 | 60 | 4,218 | 20 | 203,555 |
| | | | | | | | | | | | | 540 | | 540 |
| | | | | | | | | | | | 92 | | | 92 |
| | | | | | | | | | | | | | | - |
| | | | | | | | | | | | | | | - |
| - | - | - | - | - | - | - | - | - | - | - | 92 | - | 540 | 632 |
| ... | 28 | ... | 475 | 137 | - | - | 329 | 5,400 | 5,890 | 400 | 261 | 2,066 | 1,140 | 17,886 |
| 52,245 | 2,962 | 1,459 | 13,180 | 1,132 | ... | - | 2,931 | 33,200 | 100,680 | 4,400 | 453 | 6,284 | 1,170 | 234,178 |
| ... | ... | | ... | ... | ... | | ... | 3,780 | 750 | 560 | 600 | 3,721 | 2,151 | 11,882 |
| 8,460 | | | 5,250 | 281 | | | | 7,020 | | 320 | 75 | 2,346 | 867 | 24,619 |
| | | | | | | | | | | | | 8,433 | | 8,433 |
| 121,095 | 2,376 | 3,191 | 28,970 | 3,487 | 61,958 | 3,128 | | 10,000 | 5,570 | 2,600 | 672 | 14,864 | 61,074 | 399,710 |
| 129,555 | 2,376 | 3,191 | 34,220 | 3,768 | 61,958 | 3,128 | 13,392 | 20,800 | 6,320 | 3,480 | 1,347 | 29,364 | 64,093 | 444,644 |
| 181,800 | 5,338 | 4,650 | 47,400 | 4,900 | 61,958 | 3,128 | 16,323 | 54,000 | 107,000 | 7,880 | 1,800 | 35,648 | 65,793 | 678,822 |

(continued)

TABLE 5.1 (continued)

| Input \ Output | Final Demand | | | | | | | | Σ 25–32 | Total Output Σ 1–32 |
|---|---|---|---|---|---|---|---|---|---|---|
| | Households | | Invest-ment | Govt. Expen-diture | Rest Nepal | Wages | India | World | | |
| | Hills 25. | Terai 26. | 27. | 28. | 29. | 30. | 31. | 32. | | |
| **Intermediate Inputs** | | | | | | | | | | |
| Hill economy without services | | | | | | | | | | |
| 1. Paddy | 19,790 | – | | | | | | | 19,790 | 20,350 |
| 2. Millet | 4,374 | – | | | | | | | 4,374 | 4,440 |
| 3. Maize | 30,460 | ... | | | | | | | 30,460 | 31,020 |
| 4. Potatoes | 5,720 | 702 | | | | | 295 | | 6,717 | 8,560 |
| 5. Citrus fruits | ... | 523 | | | | | 557 | | 1,080 | 1,120 |
| 6. Medicinal herbs | – | – | | | | | 1,550 | ... | 1,550 | 1,550 |
| 7. Livestock | ... | 300 | | | | | 350 | | 650 | 9,367 |
| 8. Other agricultural products | 2,548 | ... | | | | | – | | 2,548 | 2,867 |
| 9. Brass utensils | 175 | 350 | | | 175 | | ... | | 700 | 700 |
| 10. Other products | ... | 1,230 | | | ... | | ... | | 1,230 | 1,230 |
| Σ   1–10 | 63,067 | 3,105 | | | 175 | | 2,752 | | 69,099 | 81,204 |
| Terai agriculture | | | | | | | | | | |
| 11. Paddy | ... | 81,265 | | | ... | | 2,000 | | 83,265 | 181,800 |
| 12. Wheat | – | 4,804 | | | | | | | 4,804 | 5,338 |
| 13. Oil seeds | – | 258 | | | | | | | 258 | 4,650 |
| 14. Jute | ... | 474 | | | ... | | 300 | 18,121 | 18,895 | 47,400 |
| 15. Sugarcane | – | 415 | | | | | | | 415 | 4,900 |
| 16. Livestock | | ... | | | | | | | ... | 61,958 |
| 17. Forestry | | ... | | | | | 1,200 | | 1,200 | 3,128 |
| 18. Other agricultural products | ... | 12,316 | | | ... | | 789 | | 13,105 | 16,323 |
| Σ   11–18 | | 99,532 | | | | | 4,289 | 18,121 | 121,942 | 325,497 |
| Terai industry | | | | | | | | | | |
| 19. Jute processing | ... | 270 | | | 1,890 | | 5,400 | 45,900 | 53,460 | 54,000 |
| 20. Rice and oil | ... | 73,100 | | | ... | | 33,900 | ... | 107,000 | 107,000 |
| 21. Sugar refineries | 3,000 | 4,300 | | | ... | | 488 | – | 7,788 | 7,880 |
| 22. Fruit and food processing | ... | 1,550 | | | 250 | | ... | | 1,800 | 1,800 |
| 23. Other industries | 2,300 | 12,478 | 320 | 350 | 7,300 | | 12,700 | 200 | 35,648 | 35,648 |
| Σ   19–23 | 5,300 | 91,698 | 320 | 350 | 9,440 | | 52,488 | 46,100 | 205,696 | 206,328 |
| 24. Services | 9,670 | 17,350 | 18 | 175 | 1,332 | | 11,383 | 7,979 | 47,907 | 65,793 |
| Σ   1–24 | 78,037 | 211,685 | 338 | 525 | 10,947 | | 70,912 | 72,200 | 444,644 | 678,822 |
| **Primary Inputs** | | | | | | | | | | |
| 25. Import: rest of Nepal | ... | ... | ... | ... | | | | | ... | |
| 26. Import: India | 44,000 | 55,000 | ... | ... | | | | | 99,000 | 110,882 |
| 27. Import: wages, India | | | | ... | | | | | ... | 24,619 |
| 28. Import: rest of world | ... | ... | ... | ... | | | | | | 8,433 |
| 29. Others | 2,000 | 3,000 | 30 | 2,909 | 785 | 16,300 | 3,955 | 20 | 28,999 | 428,709 |
| Σ   25–29 | 46,000 | 58,000 | 30 | 2,909 | 785 | 16,300 | 3,955 | 20 | 127,999 | 572,634 |
| Total inputs Σ 1–29 | 124,037 | 269,685 | 368 | 3,434 | 11,732 | 16,300 | 74,867 | 72,220 | 572,643 | 1,251,465 |

80

## Industrial Program

For the analysis of the industrial structure a simplified technique of industrial-complex analysis was prepared. The forward and backward linkages of the various industries were to be estimated within the framework of the input-output table.

## Dam Project

In case the irrigation project turned out to be a relevant project, an approach to determine the regional spread effects was prepared, combining cost-benefit and cost-effectiveness analysis and input-output analysis.

## Development Program for the Hills

The usual methods of empirical social research were applied, and a special questionnaire covering all essential hypotheses in suitable question form was developed.

## Formulation of Other Questionnaires

It was felt that other detailed questionnaires covering all other fields in which interviews were envisaged should also be drawn up prior to departure. Questionnaires were also developed for the following fields: Terai industry, Terai agriculture, consumer budgets, wholesale trade, and the socioeconomic situation of the Hill. All questionnaires were geared to the information requirements of the input-output table and the four formulated program hypotheses.

## Scheduling

In the period between November 15, 1971, and February 10, 1972, 13 weeks were available for field work. Precisely because the actual situation appeared to be so uncertain, it was considered necessary to draw up a clear time budget beforehand in order to ensure the required degree of flexibility during the empirical surveys and to prevent getting bogged down in difficult detailed problems.

Week 1:     Arrival and data collection in Kathmandu.

Weeks       Flight to Kosi Zone. Empirical surveys of industry and
2 to 4:     services in Biratnagar for the construction of the input-output table and review of the program hypothesis "industry." Empirical surveys in agriculture to cover the

information requirements of the input-output table and testing of the program hypothesis "dam project."

Weeks 5 to 6: Empirical survey in the Hills to cover the information requirements of the input-output table, survey of the economic and social structure of the Hills, and the economic linkages between the Hills and the Terai. Testing of the program hypotheses "transportation project" and "Hills development program."

Week 7: Continuation of the surveys in Biratnagar. In particular the collection of the industrial questionnaires that might not be completed before leaving for the Hills.

Week 8: Drawing up the draft report in Kosi Zone, identification of eventual information gaps that might remain, and closing of those gaps.

Weeks 9 to 13: Flight back to Kathmandu, presentation and discussion of the draft report with all interested bodies, further work on the selected program hypotheses, completion of the final report in permanent discussion with the Planning Commission and the ministries, presentation of the final report, and discussion of the same before leaving the country.

The idea behind this time schedule was to complete the survey work and the identification of the relevant program hypothesis by the end of the sixth week and to formulate the results for the Planning Commission by the end of the eighth week while still in the survey region. Thus, five open weeks remained for detailed work covering specific needs of the Planning Commission that could not be anticipated beforehand and that could now be tackled against the background of the insights gained in the field and submitted in report form to the Planning Commission. The crucial point was <u>the presentation of the final report and the discussion with the Nepalese decision makers before departure</u>.

## PROGRESS OF THE FIELD WORK AND INTERMEDIATE RESULTS

The talks in Kathmandu produced little additional information to that already obtained during the preparatory phase in Berlin, but they revealed that the Nepalese agencies wished to place the emphasis on the Hills in all eventual program hypotheses and wanted the team to return with concrete proposals. This was the first switch to the concentration on the subregion of the Hills.

Research Findings in the Terai

Surveys were conducted in the Terai from November 20 to December 4, 1971. They concentrated on the industrial structure of Biratnagar, the present and future demand for industrial and agricultural products, and on the socioeconomic situation in the Terai on the basis of six representative villages. The following are the principal findings.

First, the industrial structure of Biratnagar is outdated and not competitive in comparison to the larger and more modern installations in India. The jute industry, which is the leading industry, with 47 percent of all employed persons (5,200), is kept alive through an export-bonus system by which the jute dealers in Biratnagar--mostly of Indian origin--compensate for the high losses they incur through the purchase of Nepalese jute products, which are not internationally competitive in terms of cost, and their sales at subpurchase prices through an export bonus from the government of Nepal (about 60 percent of the export value) for export to hard currency countries (therefore, not to India). With this money they import high-quality industrial commodities that they can sell at a great profit in Nepal. A large proportion of these goods finds its way to India across the virtually uncontrollable 1,000 kilometer border, generally evading customs duties.

One can hardly say that the industry of Biratnagar has reached the stage of self-sustained growth. Biratnagar cannot be considered as a stimulating growth center for Kosi Zone that will generate positive development effects for the entire region. The town is without doubt the largest market for agricultural products in the region, but its industrial backward-linkage effects are limited to a few agricultural processing sectors, above all jute, rice, oil seeds, and sugarcane. There are virtually no forward linkages: Most of the industrial output is directly exported.

Second, agriculture in the Terai concentrates on rice, wheat, and jute. The farmers live on a subsistence level. The main problem confronting the farmers is how to meet their basic needs--i.e., basic foods and clothing. A surprisingly large proportion of the population is prepared--in keeping with ancient Nepalese tradition-- to supply voluntary labor for development efforts, provided that additional technical know-how, efficient management, equipment, and funds are supplied by the government.

Third, the Kankai dam program hypothesis exceeded the investment volume that may reasonably be expected for the region within the next few years. Neither had the existing project discussions reached an advanced stage, nor did a major donor country appear to be interested in financing such a project.

Fourth, the program hypothesis on industry was also not immediately relevant in view of the situation outlined above. Production and marketing conditions are unfavorable, and no investment funds have been allocated for major modernization programs in the development budget of Nepal, with the exception of the jute modernization program that is mostly financed by the Asian Development Bank in its effort to promote the production of raw jute and its industrial processing. This, however, will not bring about any major changes in the overall problem.

Finally, at this stage of the empirical surveys no light had yet been thrown on the economic and social situation in the Hills and on interrelationships between the Hills and the Terai in the Kosi Zone. Swiss development aid projects in other zones had produced the feeling that there is practically no north-south interrelationship worth mentioning, but that the trade of the Hills follows the line of the east-west hill ranges--i.e., in a transverse direction to the administrative north-south demarcation of the zones. The entire Hill area of the Kosi Zone was more or less terra incognita: Available information was practically nil.

## Research Findings in the Hills

There are no roads north of Dharan. All loads are carried on porters' backs. From December 5 to 23, the team surveyed the most important market centers--i.e., Dhankuta, Terhathum, Hille, Chainpur, Khandbari, and Tumlingtar, in addition to some selected villages with a walking distance of four hours from those market centers. It was found that a limited sample was sufficient, as the problems along the same altitude were relatively homogenous. In particular, knowledgeable persons, such as the members of the village and district administration, the elected local officials, small and big farmers, groups of farmers (village hearings), and local school teachers were interviewed.

Relatively soon it became clear that the economic and social situation in the Hills has reached a critical phase. The area lives almost exclusively on agriculture. The rice yields are higher than those of the Terai due to more intensive farming, which is, again, the result of the higher population density. These yields could be raised further if irrigation and fertilizers were available, as trial projects have shown. Other important products are seed potatoes and citrus fruit, both exported to the Terai and to India.

The main problem is lack of access to markets due to lack of transport facilities. There are no medical services. In many places there is a shortage of water for drinking and irrigation. The

agricultural output of many small farms is too low to provide sufficient food for the family.  Population has doubled in the past 40
years, and the growing population pressure has resulted in increased
pressure on the cultivated land.  The farmed terraces have en-
croached higher and higher into former forested areas, so progres-
sively less productive land is being put under cultivation at higher
costs in terms of human labor.  There is seasonal shortage of labor.
The expansion of terrace farming, and the cutting down of the for-
ests to obtain firewood has increased the damage caused by erosion
from year to year.  Due to the lack of transport facilities it is not
possible to use fertilizers, and the terraces are suffering from soil
exhaustion.  There is a growing number of people who are reluc-
tantly starting to think seriously about the necessity of migration.
The reasons for their reluctance are quite obvious--e.g., the climate of the hot plains, which is hard for the mountain tribes to bear,
and the economic difficulties that they know they will encounter in
the south.  The Terai does not have sufficient land for newcomers,
and the industry of Biratnagar cannot provide employment for all the
migrants.
      This critical situation is highlighted in the trade balance of
the Hills.  Of the total imports, amounting to Rs 49 million ($4.9
million) per annum, mainly for textiles, shoes, mustard oil, sugar,
cigarettes, salt, tea, and kerosene, * only about one-third are
financed by own exports, above all medicinal herbs, seed potatoes,
citrus fruit, butter, spices, brass utensils, live animals, and wool.†
One-third of the imports are covered by military services in the Indian or British armies (the so-called Gurkha soldiers) and by seasonal labor (mainly in India).  The remaining deficit is covered by
income from landholding in the Terai (the more well-to-do families),
and by steadily growing indebtedness to dealers in the Terai.  This
indebtedness leads sooner or later to a loss of own land and thus to
migration.
      The surveys produced the first figures ever obtained on the
economic structure of the Hills and the physical units, values, and
directions of the flow of goods and services and the flow of persons

------

      *See Table 5.1.  Rs 5.3 million from Terai industry (row total
19-25, column 3) and Rs 44 million from India (row 26, column 25).
      †In Table 5.1 only Rs 6 million is entered: namely, Rs 3.1
million to households, Terai; Rs 0.17 million to rest of Nepal; Rs
2.75 million to India (row total 1-10, columns 26, 29, 31).   After
the table had been completed a more detailed survey for the analysis of flows of goods was undertaken.  These flows could not be
ascertained statistically when the table was being constructed.

between the Hills, the Terai, and India. The flow of persons increases after the harvest in December to 40,000 in one direction (i.e., 80,000 persons in both directions), which actually leads to "traffic jams" on the porter tracks. On the whole, the team's estimates gave a total of 320,000 persons in one direction, or 640,000 persons in both directions per year.

The two major findings were as follows. First, the most urgent felt need of the Hill population is a transport facility. This is needed not only to carry production inputs, such as fertilizers, up to the Hills but also to carry agricultural products down to the markets in the south. The major bottleneck in the existing transport system is the connection between Dharan and the first market center in the Hills, Dhankuta (a distance of about 70 kilometers). The second priority is given to irrigation, where, as in the case of transport, the main objective in the eyes of the Hill population is a direct increase of agricultural production. Therefore, one hypothesis proved to be wrong; namely, that the economic situation in the Hills is more or less satisfactory and that migration could be checked through the provision of social services, such as medical care, drinking water, schools, and so on. In all interviews these services followed much lower on the list of felt needs, long after the measures required for a direct increase of agricultural yields.

## Conclusions for Development

The situation in the Hills became clear as described in the middle of December. In view of the shortage of available resources for development projects (in Nepal the majority of all development projects have to be financed through foreign aid), and in view of the fact that the Planning Commission has especially emphasized the need for program proposals on the development of the Hills, the obvious course of action for the team was to concentrate all further activities on the most urgent bottleneck in the Hill areas of the Kosi Zone--i.e., the solution of the transport problem. In operational terms this meant the analysis of the possibilities of a transport link between Dharan and Dhankuta, and in this context the alternatives of a road or a ropeway arose for discussion.

The composition of the team made it necessary to concentrate on areas that could be covered adequately by the technical qualifications of its members and that, at the same time, would offer an adequate background documentation for a policy decision in favor of the solution of the transport problem. Special emphasis was laid on the detailed analysis of the traffic flows in terms of physical units, values, and places. At the same time, there was a discussion of the readiness of the district administration and the panchayats to participate actively in the implementation of the transport project. It was found that the villagers readily offered voluntary labor. After evaluating relevant documents and experience, an economic and social prefeasibility study--a comparison of the virtues of a road versus those of a ropeway--was worked out with the aid of resident experts (see Chart 5.1). The following aspects supported the road solution: The investment costs would be 40 percent cheaper; maintenance would be even more favorable in terms of cost; the construction (unlike that of a ropeway) could be undertaken by using local unskilled labor, implying a considerable regional employment effect. Beside those aspects, most of the components needed for the construction of a ropeway would have to be imported. Road maintenance would also be labor-intensive. The highly qualified technical maintenance that would be required for a ropeway could not, under the prevailing conditions, be guaranteed. A road would have the advantage of creating direct access to the road system of the Terai, and it would bring about a direct connection down to India. North of Dhankuta an additional network of roads, some of which already exist, could be laid out at relatively low cost with the use of voluntary labor from the panchayats, so jeeps and land rovers could penetrate far beyond Dhankuta and reach remote villages on simple tracks. Thus, a Dharan-Dhankuta road would have considerable regional spread effects on the Hills north of Dhankuta. A road would be accessible along the whole alignment, whereas a ropeway, with its point-to-point system, would have no access in between. Every transport link, and in particular a road link, has a number of positive effects on several other objectives above and beyond those of production increase--e.g., quick access for social services (medical care; school buses; quick relief measures in case of natural disasters, such as floods, famine, and so on), a stronger administrative link with the remote administrative centers in the north (a civil servant has to trek for five days from Dharan to Khandbari, the northernmost administrative center), and integration effects of a social and political nature between the Hills and the Terai.

For the team the main issue was that this top-priority road project should not be deferred in favor of other less urgent projects. Therefore, an explicit negative recommendation was made at the same time--i.e., a recommendation not to implement other projects before the road project had been commenced. It was stressed that the farmers in the Hills, many of them ex-Gurkha soldiers who have traveled all over the world and received modern education, would not hesitate, as the survey showed, to exploit the chances of increasing their cash income as soon as they had a possibility of access to the markets in the south.

## CHART 5.1

### Traffic Flow, Dharan-Hills

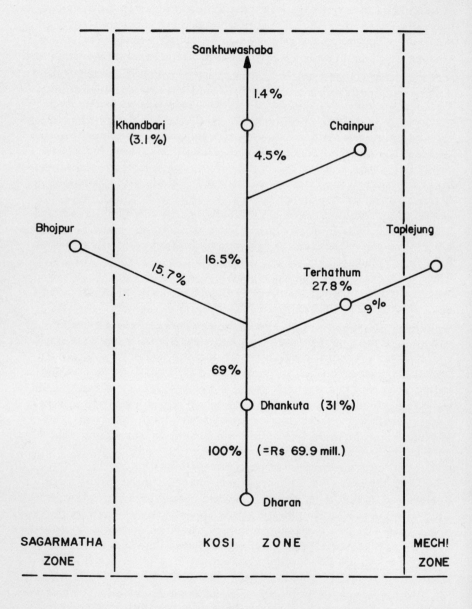

After the construction of the Dharan-Dhankuta road, development efforts should concentrate on the promotion of products that do not compete with similar products in the Terai or in North India. The latter can be cultivated at lower cost in the south. Therefore, first, an analysis of market outlets should be undertaken (this was beyond the scope of the team's work), and then the special conditions prevailing in the Hills should be exploited--e.g., the climate that favors specific products such as fruit, medicinal herbs, seed potatoes, and so forth. This will probably necessitate a change in present cropping patterns in the Hills, which, due to the present transport conditions, are oriented toward meeting the demand for basic foods. These basic foods could, however, be cultivated at lower cost in the Terai and then transported up to the Hills as soon as the transport problem has been solved, whereas the Hills could concentrate on more productive crops.

As the work proceeded it was found that a large donor country was prepared to finance the road solution. Given these political and administrative implementation aspects, the team concentrated its further activity on collecting convincing arguments in favor of this useful and feasible project and on advocating them vis-a-vis the Planning Commission and the resident representatives of potential national and international donor institutions.

These initiatives began in the first week of January 1972 in the form of a preliminary draft report to the Planning Commission after the return to Kathmandu. In the following weeks the socio-economic analysis of the region and, in particular, the input-output table were completed. This frame highlighted the problems of intraregional interdependence and thus emphasized the importance of the road project, which would connect the Hills to the north-south Dharan-Biratnagar-India road, on the one hand, and, on the other, to the East-West Highway, which will link the whole of Nepal from east to west and which is in the process of being completed.

## RESULTS OF INPUT-OUTPUT STUDY

The input-output table can also be used as a basis for the analysis of longer term development opportunities, particularly if an inverted matrix is prepared, giving total interindustry multipliers, as in Table 5.2. The intraregional interdependence between the Terai and the Hills is equally low. For example, out of a total output of Rs 69 million ($6.9 million) the Hills only supply goods worth Rs 3 million ($0.3 million) to the households in the Terai, mainly seed potatoes, foodstuffs, brass utensils, and spices; conversely, out of a total output of Rs 122 million ($12.2 million) in agriculture

TABLE 5.2

Input–Output Table of the Kosi Zone, 1969-70, Inverted Matrix

| Output / Input | Intermediate Demand Hill Economy Without Services | | | | | | | | | |
|---|---|---|---|---|---|---|---|---|---|---|
| | 1. | 2. | 3. | 4. | 5. | 6. | 7. | 8. | 9. | 10. |
| **Intermediate Inputs** | | | | | | | | | | |
| **Hill economy without services** | | | | | | | | | | |
| 1. Paddy | 1.0282 | | | | | | | | | |
| 2. Millet | | 1.0151 | | | | | | | | |
| 3. Maize | | | 1.0184 | | | | | | | |
| 4. Potatoes | | | | 1.2245 | | | | | | |
| 5. Citrus fruits | | | | | 1.0000 | | | | | |
| 6. Medicinal herbs | | | | | | 1.0000 | | | | |
| 7. Livestock | 0.1101 | | 0.1674 | 0.0536 | | | 1.0000 | 0.4117 | 0.0182 | |
| 8. Other agricultural products | | | | | | | | 1.1116 | 0.0493 | |
| 9. Brass utensils | | | | | | | | 1.0000 | | |
| 10. Other products | | | | | | | | | | 1.0000 |
| **Terai agriculture** | | | | | | | | | | |
| 11. Paddy | | | | | | | | | | |
| 12. Wheat | | | | | | | | | | |
| 13. Oil seeds | | | | | | | | | | |
| 14. Jute | | | | | | | | | 0.0002 | |
| 15. Sugarcane | | | | | | | | | | |
| 16. Livestock | | | | | | | | | | |
| 17. Forestry | | | | | | | | | | |
| 18. Other agricultural products | | | | | | | | | | |
| **Terai industry** | | | | | | | | | | |
| 19. Jute processing | | | | | | | | | 0.0004 | |
| 20. Rice husking and oil extracting | | | | | | | | | | |
| 21. Sugar refineries | | | | | | | | | | |
| 22. Fruit and food processing | | | | | | | | | | |
| 23. Wood and furniture | | | | | | | | | | |
| 24. Stainless steel | | | | | | | | | | |
| 25. Synthetic textiles | | | | | | | | | | |
| 26. Bricks and tiles | | | | | | | | | | |
| 27. Other industries | | | | | | | | | | |
| **Services** | | | | | | | | | | |
| 28. Electricity | | | | | | | | | 0.0004 | |
| 29. Jute baling | | | | | | | | | | |
| 30. Repairing works | | | 0.0001 | 0.0001 | | | | | 0.0004 | |
| 31. Transport | 0.0194 | | 0.0314 | 0.0437 | | | | 0.0046 | 0.1045 | |
| 32. Trade and other services | 0.0001 | | 0.0002 | 0.0004 | | | | | 0.0367 | |

| | | | | Intermediate Demand | | | | | | | | |
| | | | | Terai Agriculture | | | | | | | | |
| 11. | 12. | 13. | 14. | 15. | 16. | 17. | 18. | 19. | 20. | 21. | 22. | 23. |
|---|---|---|---|---|---|---|---|---|---|---|---|---|
| | | | | | | | | | | | 0.0222 | |
| 1.0436 | | | | | | | | | 0.8868 | | | |
| | 1.1112 | | | | | | | | 0.0406 | | | |
| | | 1.1291 | | | | | | | | | | |
| | | | 1.0151 | | | | | 0.5229 | 0.0002 | 0.0001 | 0.0005 | 0.0005 |
| | | | | 1.1303 | | | | | | 0.5622 | 0.0287 | |
| 0.2563 | 0.4996 | 0.2250 | 0.2570 | 0.0991 | 1.0000 | | 0.0968 | 0.1324 | 0.2259 | 0.0493 | 0.0359 | 0.0001 |
| | | | | | | 1.0000 | | | | 0.0102 | 0.0005 | 0.2965 |
| | | | | | | | 1.0534 | | | | | |
| | | | | | | | | 1.0006 | 0.0004 | 0.0002 | 0.0010 | 0.0009 |
| | | | | | | | | | 1.0000 | | | |
| | | | | | | | | | | 1.0000 | 0.0511 | |
| | | | | | | | | | | | 1.0000 | |
| | | | | | | | | | | | | 1.0000 |
| | | | | | | | | 0.0320 | 0.0003 | 0.0106 | 0.0187 | 0.0020 |
| | | | | 0.0001 | | | | 0.0101 | 0.0001 | | 0.0003 | 0.0005 |
| | 0.0057 | | 0.0101 | 0.0316 | | | 0.0215 | 0.0156 | 0.0250 | 0.0361 | 0.0519 | 0.1317 |
| | | | | 0.0002 | | | 0.0006 | 0.0506 | 0.0302 | 0.0208 | 0.0802 | 0.0725 |

(continued)

TABLE 5.2 (continued)

| Output / Input | Intermediate Demand | | | | | | | | |
|---|---|---|---|---|---|---|---|---|---|
| | Terai Industry | | | | Services | | | | |
| | 24. | 25. | 26. | 27. | 28. | 29. | 30. | 31. | 32. |
| **Intermediate Inputs** | | | | | | | | | |
| **Hill economy without services** | | | | | | | | | |
| 1. Paddy | | | | | | | | | |
| 2. Millet | | | | | | | | | |
| 3. Maize | | | | | | | | | |
| 4. Potatoes | | | | 0.0045 | | | | | |
| 5. Citrus fruits | | | | | | | | | |
| 6. Medicinal herbs | | | | 0.0002 | | | | | |
| 7. Livestock | | | | | | | | | |
| 8. Other agricultural products | | | | | | | | | |
| 9. Brass utensils | | | | | | | | | |
| 10. Other products | | | | | | | | | |
| **Terai agriculture** | | | | | | | | | |
| 11. Paddy | | | | | | | | | |
| 12. Wheat | | | | | | | | | |
| 13. Oil seeds | | | | | | | | | |
| 14. Jute | | | | 0.0002 | 0.0001 | 0.0008 | | | 0.0071 |
| 15. Sugarcane | | | | | | | | | |
| 16. Livestock | | | | 0.0206 | | 0.0002 | | | 0.0018 |
| 17. Forestry | | | 0.0125 | 0.0184 | | 0.0250 | | | |
| 18. Other agricultural products | | | | 0.2238 | | | | | |
| **Terai industry** | | | | | | | | | |
| 19. Jute processing | | 0.0001 | | 0.0004 | 0.0002 | 0.0016 | | 0.0001 | 0.0136 |
| 20. Rice husking and oil extracting | | | | | | | | | |
| 21. Sugar refineries | | | | | | | | | |
| 22. Fruit and food processing | | | | | | | | | |
| 23. Wood and furniture | | | | | | | | | |
| 24. Stainless steel | 1.0000 | | | | | | | | |
| 25. Synthetic textiles | | 1.0000 | | | | | | | |
| 26. Bricks and tiles | | | 1.0000 | | | | | | |
| 27. Other industries | | | | 1.0000 | | | | | |
| **Services** | | | | | | | | | |
| 28. Electricity | 0.0059 | 0.0158 | | 0.0031 | 1.0294 | 0.0477 | 0.0576 | 0.0003 | 0.0121 |
| 29. Jute baling | | | | | | 1.0000 | | | |
| 30. Repairing works | | | | 0.0001 | | 0.0002 | 1.0000 | 0.0033 | 0.0020 |
| 31. Transport | | 0.0001 | | 0.0333 | 0.0074 | 0.0003 | 0.0154 | 1.0000 | 0.0003 |
| 32. Trade and other services | 0.0066 | 0.0074 | | 0.0318 | 0.0149 | 0.1219 | 0.0009 | 0.0093 | 1.0008 |

and Rs 206 million ($20.6 million) in industry the Terai only supplies
commodities worth Rs 5 million ($0.5 million) to the Hills.   Table
5.1 also shows the strong economic links of the Hills and the Terai
with India, which are much stronger than the links with the rest of
Nepal.

     The table can also be used as a base for the analysis of longer-
term development opportunities.   In a first step an estimate of
import-substitution possibilities can be undertaken.   The economic
structure shows that in the Kosi Zone there are practically no possibilities for import substitution of investment goods and intermediate
industrial inputs, because the small size of the market does not permit a full utilization of the minimum technical and economic capacities required to operate such industries.   One possible development
would be the gradual replacement of industrial labor from India by
Nepalis in the course of a longer-term training program.   Regarding
final demand, diverse industrial products for daily use in households,
such as textiles, shoes, processed foods, bicycles, torches, batter-
ies, soap, kerosene, and so on, are now imported.   Again, the present size of the market in most branches does not favor a transition to
local production, especially as it would face serious competition
from the relatively efficient and low-cost production of the same
goods in India.   The survey of the industrial workers' households
and agriculture showed that, even with a 20 percent rise in income,
demand will continue to be oriented toward the daily necessities of
food and clothing.   Due to low incomes, those needs cannot be met
adequately at the moment.   Therefore, the present and future markets for industrial products in the Kosi Zone are limited.   An increase of the overall purchasing power will have to be brought about
via exports.

     In the examination of export opportunities the input-output
should be studied by row, first, to see whether present exports could
be raised and, second, to identify new export sectors in the table.   A
detailed analysis could not be undertaken, due to time and personnel
constraints.   It is, however, quite obvious that Terai industry has
considerable difficulty in competing with Indian products, insofar as
production costs are concerned.   Terai agriculture produces the
same crops as those cultivated in neighboring areas of India.   Only
certain products in the Hills--above all citrus fruit, medicinal herbs,
and seed potatoes--have specific climatic and locational advantages.
One possible course of action would be to increase exports of those
products and also to introduce other crops such as orchard fruit,
tea, and so on after the transportation problem affecting the inflow
of inputs and the outflow of products for sale has been solved.   The
export possibilities to other regions of Nepal will improve after the
traffic link via the East-West Highway has been completed.   In order

to examine all these questions, detailed and specific surveys will be necessary, especially in the field of marketing and improved agricultural production. Preliminary studies on these subjects have been commissioned by the Planning Commission.

## NOTES

1. D. P. Ojha, Dieter Weiss et al., Regional Analysis of Kosi Zone/Eastern Nepal, vols. 1 and 2 (Berlin and Kathmandu, 1972).

2. H. C. Bos and C. M. Koyck, "The Appraisal of Road Construction Projects: A Practical Example," Review of Economics and Statistics 43 (1961): 13.

PART

III

METHODS

# 6

## THE APPLICATION OF
## SOCIAL PLANNING
## METHODS IN
## REGIONAL PLANNING:
## SOUTH GWEMBE, ZAMBIA
Martin Schümer

On request of the Ministry of Rural Development of Zambia a four-man team from the German Development Institute (GDI) carried out a regional-planning survey in the Gwembe Valley, Southern Province, from October to December 1971.* The regional development program (RDP) for South Gwembe was developed on the basis of the reduced planning approach. The development strategy adopted called for increasing regional income through export-substitution, import-substitution, and complementary projects. Two principal social-planning approaches were used: the felt-needs approach and the social-information system. They were applied in two phases of the planning process: the identification of goals and the identification of complementary projects in the social sectors.

The term "social planning" in this context is used in a much broader sense than to mean planning of social sectors. Within an integrated regional-planning concept social planning has three tasks. The first is to devise measures for the motivation of the population. This can be achieved through spreading economic and social incentives, as well as through better recognition of the felt needs of the people in the planning process. The second is the creation of the prerequisites to enable integration of the population into the regional production process. This means raising labor productivity through adequate nutrition programs and through broad-based education and training for higher-skill jobs. The third task is creation of equal access to social services. In a regional context this requires that at

---

*H. Brandt, H. Kerlen, M. Schümer, and P. P. Waller, Report on the Development Possibilities of Gwembe South Region (Zambia) (Berlin: GDI, 1973).

least by the end of a planning period social services should be equally
available for people in the various parts of the region.


## THE PLANNING REGION

### Area and Population

The southern part of Gwembe District, Southern Province,
Zambia, comprises an area of approximately 2,200 square miles
and an estimated population of 45,000 persons in 1972. The Southern
Gwembe Valley is bordered on the east by Lake Kariba and on the
west by the Zambezi Escarpment (see Map 6.1).

The population of the Gwembe Valley belongs to the Tonga
tribe, one of the largest tribes in Zambia. Due to the difficulty of
access to the Gwembe Valley over the Zambezi escarpment, this
area remained untouched for a long time by modern development.
In 1959 the Kariba dam was completed, and the lake reached its
present dimensions in 1960, covering an area of more than 2,000
square miles. It required the resettlement of 50,000 people. Of
these people 34,000 were resettled on the northern bank within
Zambia, and 22,000 came to South Gwembe region, into areas that
were generally much less suited for agriculture than were those they
had inhabited before. In years of poor rainfall the people had no reserves to count on, and famine became typical for Gwembe District.
Many young Tongas left the region in search of employment. In
1972 about 10 percent of the population was employed in Rhodesia or
in other parts of Zambia.


### Economic Structure

Low rainfall and poor soils limit the natural potential of the
region, and most of the areas with better soil types are already cultivated. The agriculture in the valley is predominantly of the subsistence type, principally sorghum and millet. The only cash crop
is cotton. There are two irrigation projects, still in the trial stage
at the time of the survey: One is run by the government, uses modern machinery, and gets high yields, though at very high cost; the
other scheme, operated by the inhabitants of the surrounding villages,
with foreign technical assistance, uses simple equipment, and its
results are not so good yet as those of the first, but it is more
adapted to local conditions.

Fishing in Lake Kariba declined drastically after attaining
record levels in the first few years. In 1972 about 400 fishermen
worked the lake and sold their catch in the larger towns of the

MAP 6.1

Geographical Location of South Gwembe Region

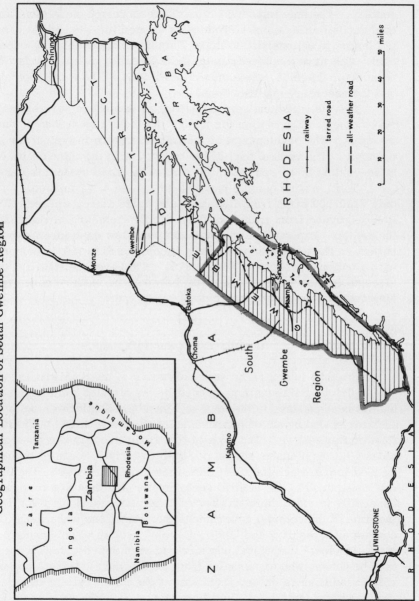

country. The only important mineral resource of the region is the coal deposit at Maamba. Production started in 1968 and its capacity is planned to be extended to make Zambia independent of Rhodesian coal. The mine employed a total of 760 workers, but very few came from South Gwembe, since only a small part of the local population had the necessary qualifications.

Private trade and service activities are characterized by low development. The reason for this is the lack of cash income outside the mine. The development of the infrastructure is typical for a dual economy. The central part of the region, with the mine as its center, is accessible by tarred road; the rest of the road system is unreliable.

Total income outside Maamba amounted to $2 million. Of this only $160,000 came from livestock and agriculture, whereas $1 million originated from transfers from family members working outside the region. Especially striking is the very low cash income in agriculture. The estimated per capita income of $130 (1971) compares with a national average of $606 (1970). This average figure, however, gives no indication of the disparity between the modern core area of Maamba and the rest of the region.


Administrative Institutions


Gwembe is one of the seven districts of the Southern Province. The district administration, headed by the district commissioner, has its headquarters in the town of Gwembe. South Gwembe is a subdistrict headed by an assistant district secretary (ADS) with his offices in Sinazongwe. The area of the subdistrict Sinazongwe coincides with the planning region of South Gwembe. South Gwembe is divided into two chieftancies: Mwemba and Sinazongwe. The chiefs are recognized by the central government, and they are responsible especially for the administration of traditional local justice. During the time of the colonial government their functions were more important as a result of the "indirect-rule" system of government.

The local traditional administration is represented by the village headmen, who are usually from among the elders. As a general rule, headmen are chosen from among the more well-to-do farmers. The headmen are elected, and they are the trusted representatives of the villagers. They are still the organizers of communal work, which is a typical high-prestige undertaking. They are the main link to the chief, and at the same time the representatives of the chief in the village, because their election has to be approved by the chief. The government tries to communicate its plans and orders to the people through the headmen system.

A parallel system of administration is the rural council (GRC), located in Munyumbwe in Central Gwembe. It consists of 60 ward councillors who are elected by the people in their wards on a party ticket. The GRC has local duties, such as maintenance of rural roads. To finance its operations it collects levies from traders, charges for services, and receives grants and loans from the Ministry of Local Government, which controls its operations.

In every district a district development committee has been created as an advisory body. Each committee is composed of the representatives of the various ministries operating in the district and is headed by the district commissioner. As a coordinating institution for all development activities in South Gwembe, a subcommittee of the district development committee was established. It consists of the district commissioner, the assistant district commissioner, representatives of sectoral ministries, the two chiefs of the area, and representatives of a German team of experts who are implementing development projects in the field of agriculture, handicrafts, and infrastructure.

An important factor in the political structure of Gwembe was the rather strong alienation between the local elite (ward councillors, headmen, and so on) and the central government. This attitude had a strong economic basis, because the Gwembe Tonga lost their main sources of income through decisions taken at the center. First, the construction of the Kariba dam destroyed the winter gardens along the Zambezi river, which were the main basis for the most important cash crop, tobacco. Second, the closing of the Zambian border with Rhodesia cut off one of the few possibilities of earning income outside the region. These two factors strengthened the affiliation of the local elite with the former opposition party, before Zambia became a one-party state. South Gwembe was represented in parliament by a member of the opposition party. Due to these circumstances, any government program was likely to face strong resistance from the local elite.

## THE IDENTIFICATION OF GOALS

In the case of South Gwembe region an analysis of the political structure showed that there were three clearly distinct opinion-formation and decision levels: the central government and the district administration; the level of the regional elites, comprising the ward councillors as members of the district council and the village leaders; and the level of the farmers. Therefore, goals had to be identified at all three levels.

## The Goals of the Government

The evaluation of Zambia's First National Development Plan (1966-70) demonstrated a growing discrepancy between the development of income in the favored areas along the line of rail and in the rest of the country. Therefore, the Second Plan (1972-76) laid special emphasis on the development of rural areas in order to generate cash income there.

The South Gwembe region was regarded by the government as a special problem area due to the resettlement of the population after the completion of the Kariba hydroelectric dam. Therefore, South Gwembe could be considered for concentrated promotion. The Ministry of Rural Development emphasized a development strategy for South Gwembe to increase cash income by concentrating on programs for the agricultural and related sectors. After a brief regional analysis, this was extended to the coal-mining and fishing sectors, owing to their high development potential.

## The Goals of the Regional Elite

During the first stay of the planning team in the region meetings were held with members of the technical departments of the government machine, with ward councillors, local tradesmen, party representatives, chiefs, elders, and headmen in each of the main chieftancies. The administration was still identified with resettlement, a fact that was widely exploited by the opposition party to discredit every development program in the region. The government party was therefore extremely unpopular among the villagers, and its organizers were regarded as representatives of "foreign interests." Technical assistants and sometimes school teachers (representing a very mobile group), alienated from the local people by education, often tribal origin, lifestyle, and residence, were regarded by the local population as sympathizing with the government party. Many of those realized the advantage to associate themselves with the government party to gain local power and influence. But they clearly favored the programs of the government in the region that would strengthen their position--for example, improvement of educational facilities for their children to ensure the technical superiority of their strata.

A very strong position was held by the shopkeepers and traders. They monopolized, to some degree, communications with the modern economy. They were able to dictate prices for simple consumer goods due to the absence of any competition in the villages, and they controlled the transport of goods and people. They feared that any major economic development program would deprive them of their

unique position as middlemen.  One of the measures demanded by
these local opinion leaders was the construction of a secondary
school in the region.  This was considered to be indispensable if the
region was to occupy a stronger position within the country as a
whole.  Only through such an institution of learning would it be possible for the people from the region to occupy a larger number of
important posts in the economy and the administration.

The chiefs were regarded by the local population as an instrument of the central administration.  During the resettlement the
chiefs exploited their position to reserve the best land in the uplands
of the valley.  The local population tried to avoid the continuing control of the chiefs by addressing itself to the representatives of the
opposition party.

The elders had gained control of a large part of the newly distributed land during resettlement.  Due to the cash payment received,
they were able to recruit more labor, and this in turn enabled them
to enlarge their fields and to maintain their economic and social position.  As a result, they have a strong aversion to all measures,
such as resettlement (even within South Gwembe region itself) or
large-scale irrigation projects, that would involve the movement of
population and a partial new distribution of land.

In general, it became obvious during the official meetings with
the representatives of the regional elite that their views were strongly
influenced by their critical attitude toward the government and their
desire to maintain their present power, although the reasons given
for their resistance were stated in terms of power.  The local elites
felt that more should be invested in the social services.  The highest
priority was given to social programs, in particular the expansion
of schools and the extension of health services.  The improvement
of these social services was considered a crucial requirement for
the general development of a region, as it seemed the only means of
preventing the continuous migration of the local entrepreneurial
groups from the valley.  In the meetings of the village headmen
great emphasis was placed on the importance of distributing social
services equally among the different population centers--i.e., there
was a demand for a policy that would locate social services directly
in the villages instead of concentrating them in regional centers.  The
local elite would benefit directly from those services, and at the
same time the services would ensure the support of the local population without endangering the power structure in the villages.

## The Goals of the Villagers

The felt needs of the village population were identified by means
of interviews in conjunction with the empirical survey of farm units.

The questions aimed at finding out what the villagers thought about
the possibility of village development and the improvement of the
agricultural situation, how they thought these goals could be achieved,
and what, in their opinion, the government could do toward that end.

It was found that priority was given to the increase of cash income, whereas the improvement of social services played a less important role. They felt that the best way to achieve this was to introduce measures for improvement in existing farms (better draft
oxen, fertilizers, seed, and so forth); less weight was attached to the
extension of land under cultivation, or to the initiation of large-scale
irrigation programs. Only a small fraction of the farmers felt that
an extension of the present subsistence agriculture would be a possible way of improving their standard of living. Some experts from
the central government had advocated the improvement of the prevailing farming techniques without including the introduction of new
crops. The farmers, however, realized that they would have no cash
returns to pay for inputs, such as fertilizers, repair of appliances,
oil for pumps, and so on, and that they would not achieve a lasting
improvement in their standard of living.

The attitude of the farmers in their expectation of government
aid was quite logically directed toward the goal of income increase.
Measures to improve cash income headed the list with 56 percent of
the respondents, whereas social services in the field of health and
education were only mentioned by 6 percent.


The Derivation of a Development Strategy

The analysis of the goals of the government and the felt needs
of the local elite and the villagers demonstrated the existence of
fundamental conflicts. A regional-growth strategy aimed at increasing incomes of the rural population would definitely be supported by
the government and would also be accepted by the villagers. On the
one hand, if it resulted in major intraregional population movements
(i.e., through irrigation projects, expansion of service centers, and
so on), it would meet with strong resistance from the local elite.
On the other hand, advocating a development strategy based on programs in the social sectors only (schools, health services, and so
on) was not feasible, because it meant increased government subsidies with no end in sight. Such a course the government was
neither willing nor able to take.

Therefore, the only feasible strategy was to increase the incomes of the rural population and to include complementary social
programs, inasmuch as they were necessary for the functioning of
the income-generating projects and for the collaboration of the local
elite. Another constraint to a pure-growth strategy was the necessity

to aim at an equal distribution of programs between the different subregions within South Gwembe.  This implied that social programs had
to be designed especially for those marginal subregions in which
income-oriented projects were not feasible due to the lacking resource
potential.

## THE IDENTIFICATION OF PROJECTS
## IN THE HEALTH SECTOR

### The Social-Information System

The method approach used for identifying programs in the education and health sectors was the application of a social-information
system.  For our purposes, the working of this method is demonstrated in the health sector only.

The point of departure was a set of indicators as an instrument
to measure specific needs in subregions, on the one hand, by com-
paring the region with the national average and, on the other hand,
by conducting intraregional comparisons to uncover those marginal
areas that had the greatest deficiency of services.  The selected indicators point to social problems that are not immediately obvious
when income is the primary indicator of well-being.  One reason for
identifying meaningful social indicators is the desire to give a more
complete picture of the socioeconomic situation, especially in marginal areas.

The most common approach is a simple comparison of per-
centage differences expressed in selected indicators.  No attempt
was made to identify the structure behind the observed phenomena.
Indicators have to represent socioeconomic problems, not only structural characteristics.  Therefore, the only indicators that can be
used are those that have some theoretical basis to discriminate between two subregions.  Indicators that were likely to be closely inter-
correlated had to be eliminated.  One possibility was to establish a
mean regional profile and to observe the way in which a subregion
deviates from that profile.

A flexible operational information system, adapted to the specific needs of the planning region, has to monitor development trends
and the impact of government activities or programs on the devia-
tions of these trends.  But the standards set as objectives for planning are rather seldom scientifically convincing and are more the
result of political bargaining processes.  In South Gwembe the point
of departure for the planning of the social programs was the assumption that the sectoral indicators, in this case the health standards of
the region, should reach the level of the national average.  To this
end, a comparison of selected indicators in the field of health was

undertaken between the national average of Zambia as a whole and the Gwembe region, in order to identify those fields in which the figures for the region lay below the national average. A subregional comparison was then carried out in order to ascertain the most urgent needs in the subregions.

## The Derivation of Meaningful Health Indicators

The indicators of a health information system had to be sufficiently broad in their conceptional framework to be used in the planning of different health programs but manageable enough to be made available in a short time by a small team for planning purposes. The health information system had to be program-oriented--that is, flexible enough for the planning of broad programs, while disaggregated enough to be applicable for the planning process of specific health services on the subregional or local level. The system had to combine health characteristics and demographic and socioeconomic data to arrive at estimations of the composition and the likely development trends of population groups that require specific services. The following indicators are those that were readily available from provincial, regional, and local data files, in combination with data from household surveys.

1.  Demographic and economic indicators
    1.1.  Size of household
    1.2.  Age-sex composition of household
    1.3.  Annual population increase
    1.4.  General fertility rate
    1.5.  Percent of population under five years of age
    1.6.  Dependency rate
    1.7.  Child-rearing index (children under 14 years of age per head of household)
    1.8.  Elderly population
    1.9.  Percent of population in broad occupational groups
    1.10. Percent of population per income groups
    1.11. Percent of population unemployed

2.  Community health indicators (these refer to the prevalence of the health status of a given group)
    2.1.  Mortality
    2.2.  Morbidity
    2.3.  Incidence of specific diseases
    2.4.  Health status of mother and children

On a local level some of this information (for example the infant mortality rate, the crude death rate, specific death rates concerning special groups) is not available. But even in marginal areas it is possible to observe substitute indicators, such as the caloric and protein deficiencies of children of specific age groups.

3. Accessibility of health services
   3.1. Existing installations (comprising government, church, voluntary organization, private institutions)
   3.2. Outpatient clinic facilities
   3.3. Catchment area per health institution
   3.4. Catchment population per health institution
   3.5. Population/bed ratio
   3.6. Mobile health units (e.g., immunization teams)
   3.7. Outpatients per day per health institution
   3.8. Inpatients per day per health institution
   3.9. Prenatal and under-five clinics per specific age groups
   3.10. Median distance to nearest health institutions

4. Health manpower indicators
   4.1. Physicians, by type of specialist per unit of population
   4.2. Ratio of nurses per patients
   4.3. Paramedical staff per patients
   4.4. Other health-related manpower per unit of population (like community development workers related to health services)

5. Health facility use
   5.1. Number of admissions in hospital per day
   5.2. Number of patient days
   5.3. Average daily census of hospital population
   5.4. Occupancy index
   5.5. Average cost of hospital day
   5.6. Routine physical examinations concerning specific population groups in a given catchment area
   5.7. Medical examinations concerning specific population groups in a given catchment area
   5.8. Hospital visits concerning specific population groups in a given catchment area
   5.9. Hospital admittances
   5.10. Medical care sought by population groups in subareas
   5.11. Accessibility of services per subarea
   5.12. Average waiting time per facility

### The Sources of Health-Information Indicators

The source for demographic and socioeconomic information was contained in the census. But the census was carried out only once a decade, and the data for population estimates in subregions were not very reliable due to out- and inmigration. Thus, these data had to be supplemented by a small area survey.

Data of health institutions, health facility use, and health manpower are normally readily available from the offices of the provincial or district medical officers--for example, in the form of hospital records. But in most cases this information excludes data to be obtained from voluntary or religious organizations active in the health field.

In any case, official statistics have to be updated and interpreted by intensive interviews with experts or data derived from household interviews conducted in the planning area. Such a survey could contain data on demographic and socioeconomic characteristics of the population health status, health utilization, satisfaction with health services, and barriers to services access.

### The Transformation of Indicators into Program Planning

The selected indicators served as measurement and planning data for program identification. The individual planning steps may be expressed in terms of the following list of successive questions.

1. What is the present level of development in terms of the above-mentioned indicators?

2. To what extent does the level of development in the planning region under discussion lie below or above the national average?

3. Which subarea of the planning region lies below or above the average level of development of the planning region?

4. Which level of development is considered to be the target that the national level of development should reach at the end of the planning period (operationalized, quantified political goals at the macro level)?

5. How much below the target national average level of development envisaged for the end of the planning period is the average level of development of the planning region?

6. Is it intended to raise the present level of development of the planning region to the present national average level of development by the end of the planning period? Further, is there even a possibility of raising it to the target national average level of

development envisaged for the end of the planning period? (Budget
restrictions, regional priorities, and additional political constraints
should be taken into account.)

7. According to which of the selected indicators and their
relative levels of development, as against (a) the average of the
planning region and (b) the national average, and in which subareas
of the planning region has the greatest need been calculated?

8. What is the calculated cost measured against unit costs
per planning unit (i.e., cost of a dispensary) in terms of the calculated need?

9. Which institutions will participate in the program? What
is their share of the costs? At which point in the planning period do
they enter the program?

10. How big is the gap in the costs resulting from the difference between the calculated need and the amount earmarked for this
purpose by the individual institutions?

As the first step in the identification process of health programs
the accessibility of the present health services in the region was
checked. The number of people served by each health unit and the
catchment area of each unit was calculated. In 1971 the population
of South Gwembe depended on six health subcenters: Sinazongwe
(serving 12,500 inhabitants), Siatwinda (10,000), Malima (10,000),
Siameja (6,000), Maamba (4,500), and Kafwambila (2,000).

In the second step the level of accessibility of health services
reached in South Gwembe was compared with the national-average
standards--for example, in the field of health manpower. In 1971
the level of services in South Gwembe was far below the national
average. The population/service ratios were as follows: doctor
ratio, 1/44,100 (national average, 9,185); medical assistant ratio,
1/4,900 (4,900); dresser ratio, 1/6,300 (4,048); nurses (midwives)
ratio, 1/14,700 (2,127).

In the third step the population distribution in the South Gwembe
region was surveyed in order to identify the subregions with the least
accessibility to services. As a result, three areas were identified:
the subregions Sinazeze (population 4,500), Sulwegoonde (3,500), and
Siankuku (2,200).

In the fourth step the data on demographic characteristics of
the population in the South Gwembe region were then applied as planning indicators to compare the distribution of health services per
1,000 inhabitants in the planning region with the national average.
By applying the national standards, the general regional demand
until the end of the planning period (of the second National Development Plan) was identified. In the planning area there were 57

hospital beds available; thus, a rate of 1.2 beds per 1,000 inhabitants had been achieved. On the basis of the population growth rate of 2.8 percent and by applying the national-average standard of Zambia, the additional number of beds required until the end of the plan period was estimated. Statistically, one member of the senior medical staff served 4,500 inhabitants, but in reality 28,000 persons were covered by three medical assistants and three dressers. Almost half of the senior medical staff was concentrated in the mining town of Maamba. Due to this subregional inequality, another seven medical assistants (or dressers) were demanded.

In the fifth and sixth steps it was obvious that, due to budget restrictions, the planning standards for the region could at best be the same as the national standards already reached at the beginning of the planning period. Proposed programs had the aim to lower the gap in such a way that the level of services in the region at the end of the planning period would reach at least the present national average. Applying the national-average standards to be reached at the end of the planning period as planning targets for South Gwembe would have resulted, for example, in a threefold increase of bed capacity--a politically unrealistic planning figure.

The seventh planning step required the greatest amount of detailed information. Data on demographic characteristics were again used to get some indications on the kind of services that should be provided in the region and the subregions. Approximately 45,000 people lived in the South Gwembe area. The average household consisted of 7.2 persons; 19 percent of the population was made up of children under five years of age; 56 percent of the population was below 15 years of age; the high birth rate of 2.8 percent, the low average life expectancy, and the high infant mortality rate of 18 percent resulted in a high dependency rate. South Gwembe contains 140 villages. On an average, South Gwembe had 30 to 40 families per village. Approximately 9,000 children under five years of age had to be covered by preventive medical campaigns. An average of 10 to 50 children under five years of age had to be looked after in every village.

Given these demographic characteristics, it was obvious that the health services had to strengthen preventive medical care. Additional information was available from the farm unit survey that contained data on malnutrition in the region and on attitudes toward preventive medicine. The per capita calorie intake amounted to 1,700-1,800, compared to the Zambian national average of 2,300. The per capita protein intake was 50-60 grams (Zambian average 60). Cases of malnutrition and deficiency diseases were almost equally distributed between the subregions, except in Siameja area with its extremely poor conditions.

The continuous extension of preventive medicine--for example, through under-five clinics--is especially obstructed by the insufficiency of information to the local population on the function of preventive medicine. Twenty-one percent of the heads of households questioned in the farm unit survey did not know of any measure of preventive medicine. Only 7 percent mentioned vaccinations or nutritional or hygienic measures.

The planning of programs in the South Gwembe region was carried out according to two alternatives of finance and personnel. Alternative I contained a minimum program package; in alternative II additional government funds for programs and services were expected. Due to those budget limitations, the following programs in the health sector were proposed (see Table 6.1): in alternative I one health subcenter and eight health posts; in alternative II three health subcenters and eight health posts. It was now necessary to decide in which of the already identified subregions, according to each alternative, additional services should be provided.

The kind of population characteristics, the dispersed locality of the villages in the region, and the collected information on malnutrition and attitudes toward preventive medicine made it necessary to provide for health posts as additional instruments of preventive medical care in both planning alternatives. These health posts were to be located between the different catchment areas of the health subcenters. In order to decide on the locality with the most urgent need in which a health subcenter should be built, additional data, except for those on population distribution, had to be taken into account. Information on the pattern of diseases and on the present level of preventive medical services in the different subregions were taken as additional planning indicators.

The incidence and occurrence of the main diseases and its subregional comparison demonstrated that malaria, as the most frequently recorded disease, had affected mainly the areas of Maamba (50 percent of the population), Siameja (13 percent of the population), and Kafwambila (12 percent of the population). A high incidence of measles was again found in Kafwambila, Maamba, and Siameja. The underrecording of the incidence of diseases in rural areas gave, however, a distorting picture, with the Maamba area seeming to be the only township with a sophisticated medical system.

Of the child population under five years of age 21 percent had attended under-five clinics at least once. Twenty-four percent of the children were vaccinated against smallpox; 21 percent against first triple antigen; 20 percent against measles. Therefore, the need of the expansion of preventive measures was obvious, especially in two subareas, as demonstrated in a subregional comparison.

## TABLE 6.1

### Proposed Programs for South Gwembe

|  | Type of Program[a] | Total Costs[b] |
|---|---|---|
| **Alternative I** | | |
| 1. Small-scale irrigation projects (vegetables) | imp. + exp. | 44,000 |
| 2. Medium-scale irrigation (rice) | exp. | 112,000 |
| 3. Medium-scale irrigation (bananas) | exp. | 116,000 |
| 4. Agricultural experimental programs (dryland) | compl. | 38,000 |
| 5. Agricultural trial programs (irrigation) | compl. | 114,000 |
| 6. Improved fish transport | imp. + exp. | 128,000 |
| 7. Improved fish marketing | imp. + exp. | |
| 8. Increased fish production | exp. | 90,000 |
| 9. Production of burnt bricks | imp. | 124,000 |
| 10. Rural crafts centers | imp. | 120,000 |
| 11. Lakeshore tourism | imp. + exp. | 100,000 |
| 12. Professional training | compl. | 270,000 |
| 13. One health subcenter, eight health posts | compl. | 64,000 |
| 14. One lower primary and one upper primary school | compl. | 110,000 |
| 15. Well-construction unit | compl. | 106,000 |
| 16. Regional-planning unit | compl. | 100,000 |
| | | 1,636,000 |
| | | |
| **Alternative II** | | |
| 17. Large-scale irrigation | exp. | 600,000 |
| 18. Local road-construction unit | compl. | 820,000 |
| 19. Maamba hospital | imp. + compl. | 1,400,000 |
| 20. Maamba secondary school | imp. + compl. | 880,000 |
| 21. Low-cost-housing scheme | compl. | 128,000 |
| 22. Two additional health subcenters | compl. | 96,000 |
| 23. Four additional primary schools | compl. | 180,000 |
| | | 4,104,000 |

[a]Imp., import-substitution program; compl., complementary program; exp., export program.

[b]Initial five years, rough estimate in dollars.

112

In the eight step, according to alternative I, the construction of one health subcenter would have resulted in total investments of $28,000, applying unit-cost calculations of the Ministry of Health. The staff requirements of a standard health subcenter created some $5,520 per year and some $1,680 per year as expenditure for drugs. In addition, the creation of eight health posts resulted in another $7,200 construction cost in case of self-help implementation. In alternative II the grand total for three health subcenters would have amounted to capital cost of $83,400 and recurrent staff costs of $11,940 per year. The cost for the health posts were the same as in alternative I.

In the ninth and tenth steps the program of alternatives I and II had to be carried out by the Ministry of Health, in this case by the provincial medical officer. It was suggested that the building of health posts and the program of nutrition education as part of the preventive health measures would be supervised and financed by a German team that managed an irrigation project in the region and that intended to expand its activities. For each alternative it was decided at which phase these two mentioned institutions had to take over their part of the program.

The programs were selected on the basis of three criteria: maximum number of persons reached by the services (in subregions with extreme need); subregional equality, if these programs could be combined with programs from other sectors; and special need for social programs, if economic projects could not be located in a subregion. According to budget alternative I, the proposed health subcenter should be located in Sinazeze, where the greatest number of inhabitants, some 4,500 people, could be served, and where the program in the health sector may have the greatest influence on and possibility of combination with other programs, especially in agriculture (see Table 6.1).

In those areas where farming techniques are highly labor-intensive, preventive measures and general medical care, as provided by health subcenters and health posts, can lead to higher agricultural output and, consequently, to growing income. This means that planning of social programs can be a precondition for the overall development of a region, particularly in terms of creating prerequisites for raising employment and income.

Budget alternative II allowed the building of two additional health subcenters in the region. According to this alternative, the project selection process is shown with the example of the proposed health subcenter Siankuku. This was a central place in a resettlement area. The economic living conditions of the remaining people were extremely difficult. The agricultural potential of the area was the poorest in the whole region. The provision of social services

could help to stabilize the remaining population and lower outmigration.  The nearest health subcenter was very far away (19 miles).
The pattern of diseases demonstrated the marginal need of medical
care in this area especially.  The results of preventive medical services were the lowest obtained from all villages.

By the planning steps discussed, target areas were determined
and programs for additional services planned.  Social complementary
programs were based on three criteria:  coordination with sector
priorities at the national level; priority in extremely backward subregions; and expected indirect influence on productivity increase.
As a next step of planning, the results of this selection process were
compared with the goals of the local elites and with the felt needs of
the population.

# 7

**BASIC ISSUES IN
THE ELABORATION OF
AN INTERREGIONAL
INPUT-OUTPUT TABLE:
AREQUIPA, PERU**
Peter P. Waller

This chapter is based on the findings of two field study groups
sent by the German Development Institute (GDI) to Southern Peru in
1969/70 and 1970/71.[1] The objective of the groups was to assist the
regional planning authority ORDESUR in establishing an interregional
input-output table as a basis for regional planning. Thus, the group
was not directly involved in action-oriented planning but rather was
to collect experience with what can be one of the most important instruments for action-oriented planning.

Input-output tables can serve four major functions: as general
framework for regional statistics; as a tool to identify regional production opportunities; as a tool to investigate regional effects of new
projects (see Chapter 5); as a tool to maximize spread effects of a
growth pole for the development of its hinterland. The fourth function was the major aspect of the Arequipa table. Arequipa plays an
important role within the national strategy for regional development
in Peru. It is considered a growth pole, and its spread effects are
to become one of the major factors in the development of Southern
Peru, one of the lagging regions of the country. Therefore, an interregional input-output table seemed to be the best tool to identify
city-hinterland relationships as a basis for a regional development
policy that would try to maximize such spread effects.

In contrast to the abundance of literature on theoretical aspects
of input-output analysis, there are very few studies on methods for
constructing and filling out an input-output table, especially in the
situation of a lagging region in a developing country. This is one of
the reasons for the almost complete lack of simple tables for such
regions. Another reason is the belief that even simple input-output
tables require a tremendous amount of statistical data or, in the absence of data, an unsurmountable amount of empirical work. This

chapter will indicate the major steps in the elaboration of a regional input-output table as a tool in action-oriented planning and propose some new methods to solve conceptual problems of accounting in the public sector and within supraregional organizations.

CONCEPTUAL ISSUES

Delineation of the Region

The investigation was focused on the Southern Region of Peru (see Map 7.1). This region had already been selected by the National Planning Institute of Peru (INP) as one of the four national planning regions, and had been delineated on the basis of functional links between Arequipa and nearby departamentos. This delineation, which reflected as well a historic regional tradition on the part of the population, was later confirmed by a graph analysis of Arequipa's area of influence, based upon migration movements and telephone calls.

The survey region has an area of 317,000 square kilometers, or 24.6 percent of the total area of Peru. In 1964 the population amounted to 2.5 million inhabitants, or 25.3 percent of the population of the country. The region stretches across the three natural zones of Peru: the desert-like coast (Costa), the Andes region (Sierra), and the tropical forest region (Selva). In 1961 the GNP of the entire region amounted to 10 billion soles ($400 million) and made up 19 percent of the national GNP.

The per capita income in some of the departamentos in the Andes only reaches 40 to 50 percent of the national average. These regions are thus among the poorest in Peru. The coastal departamentos achieve figures above the average on account of the mining sector (mostly copper), irrigated agriculture, and the city of Arequipa. In all the departamentos there is a high migration to the capital city, Lima.

Since the Arequipa table was conceived as an interregional input-output table to identify the spread effects of a growth pole, a further internal delineation between "region I" (city of Arequipa), and "region II" (hinterland of Arequipa) was required. As the city of Arequipa lies in a small river oasis and is surrounded on all sides by uninhabited desert areas, this internal delineation posed no specific problem.

MAP 7.1

Delineation of South Peru Region

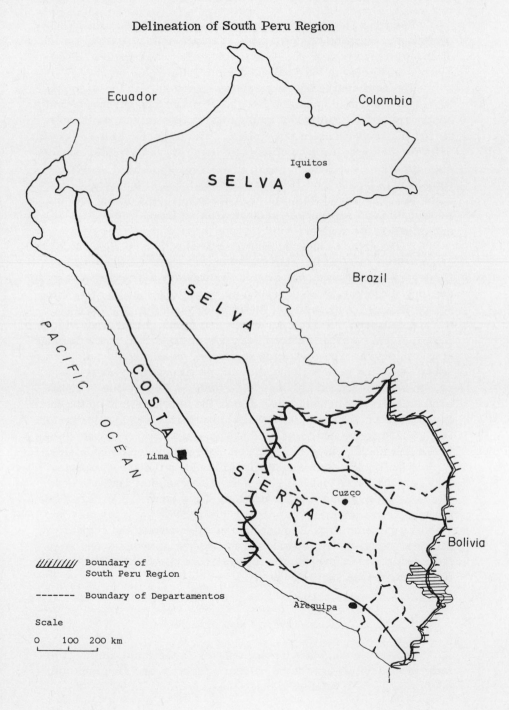

Ecuador

Colombia

Iquitos

S E L V A

Brazil

S E L V A

PACIFIC

COSTA

OCEAN

Lima

SIERRA

Cuzco

Bolivia

Arequipa

///////// Boundary of
South Peru Region

------- Boundary of Departamentos

Scale

0   100  200 km

## Delineation of Sectors

The first step is to determine the number of sectors. The limited investigation capacity made it impossible to exceed a total of about 30 matrix sectors, or 15 sectors for each region. These figures only refer to the final table (see Table 7.3, infra).

The next step is the delineation of sectors. In the Arequipa table the criteria of homogeneity, the absolute importance of the sector (measured against its gross total output value), and the expected interdependence were applied. The criterion of homogeneity calls for the classification of as many sectors as possible, but this classification is difficult to make if the total number of sectors is limited. Therefore, at first the sectors listed in the official Peruvian statistics were taken, and they were then aggregated into the manageable and appropriate number, taking into account their output values in the region.

In the primary and secondary activities official figures on the gross output value of the individual sectors were available before field work commenced, but data on the tertiary activities were very scarce. However, it was reasonable to assume that this was the sector in which important interactions between the city and its hinterland occurred. Therefore, wholesale trade, retail trade, transportation and services sectors were set up according to the homogeneity criterion. The remaining sectors--"government" and "households"--are not generally included in the transactions matrix but rather in the marginal columns and rows, as their value is considered to be fixed autonomously. But if the accent is laid on the interdependence between the city and its hinterland, these sectors must find a place in the matrix. For instance, transfer of payments between households plays an important role in developing countries.

Finally, the conventional final demand columns--"exports," "investment," and "central government"--remain. Imports and depreciation are shown in the primary input rows. In order to keep the transfer of payments out of the import rows, a separate row, "factor payments," was included for people outside the region. This covers all the remittances of dividends, interests, and so on from industrial enterprises in the entire region to households and firms outside the survey region.

## Accounting in the Trade Sectors

Before we can start making entries in the table, some problems of accounting have to be solved. First, a decision must be taken whether the value of transactions should be in terms of producers' prices or market prices.  In the Arequipa table producers' prices were adopted, in accordance with general practice.

Another problem is accounting in the trade sectors, which has a direct influence on the identification of city-hinterland interdependence.  In principle, one may have gross accounting or net accounting.  In gross accounting trade is treated like any other sector.  In net accounting only the trade margin--i.e., the difference between the sales value and the purchase value of the commodity--is recorded, and the commodity itself is accounted directly from the producer to the consumer.  Gross accounting gives more realistic coverage of interregional interdependence, but technical relationships between the supplier and the recipient are concealed, and the input-output table can therefore no longer be used as a forecasting tool.  For this reason net accounting was applied.

## Accounting in the Public Sector

In most input-output tables the accounting of the output of the public sector does not lead to any problems, since the government does not appear as a "producing" sector in the matrix.  However, interregional tables intended for application in regional planning must include the public sector that appears in the form of administration, schools, hospitals, and so on, and the problem of assessing the output of the public sector thus arises.  The inputs in this sector, such as salaries, materials, and so on, are not very different from the inputs in other sectors.

The output of the government does not usually have a market value; it is not paid by the recipient but by the taxpayer.  The costs of school education in Peru, for instance, are not covered by parents in the form of fees but by the central government in the form of grants.  If, on the one hand, the output were to be accounted in the same way as in the other sectors--i.e., on the basis of actual payments--the result would be an output from the schools in Arequipa to the central government--an absurd result. *  If, on the other hand, the services of the government were to be ignored, important interregional interrelationships, such as the hospital and university services provided by the city to the hinterland, would not be covered.  But the development of a region can be influenced just as greatly by the creation of a university as by the establishment of a factory.

---

*The central government "pays" for the hospital services, because the entire budget of the hospital is subsidized from the national budget.

Therefore, a system of direct accounting was developed for the Arequipa table. It is based on the assumption that the households are the real beneficiaries of public services. They are thus the recipients of the output of the public sector, which is assessed at the costs entered in the budgets (e.g., hospitals, university, and so on). As public institutions do not calculate on the basis of profit, it is justified to identify costs with inputs.

## Coverage of Supraregional Institutions

Many of the interregional transactions take place within large supraregional enterprises and are very difficult to identify statistically. For instance, the head office of the railways is in Arequipa, but there are stations and repair workshops in the hinterland; large commercial firms in Arequipa have branch offices in small towns in the hinterland.

In the 1963 trade census the branch offices were treated as independent firms. Even in the direct interviews the data on certain firms were divided according to head office and branches. However, this meant that a certain proportion of the interdependence was not incorporated in the calculation. The head offices of the firms provide a number of "central services" to the branches, such as central management, joint advertising, transactions with banks and public authorities, and so on, which are generally not visible in the cost calculations of the branch offices. Theoretically, they are compensated by a higher profit, which the branch offices transfer to the central office. But as it was seldom possible in practice to ascertain the exact amount of the profits, a figure of 10 percent was computed from the total input of the branch offices and accounted as "administrative services" provided by the central office in Arequipa to the branch offices in the hinterland. This method of determining "intraenterprise interactions" is still very unsatisfactory and can only be improved by having very detailed and precise interviews.

## COVERAGE OF DATA

### Strategy of Data Collection

Input-output calculation is always based on estimates. Unlike directly collected population or transport statistics, it can never be as accurate. One can only derive cautious estimates from the largest possible amount of data and indicators.

In principle, data can be obtained both directly and indirectly. In indirect data collection a distinction must be drawn between the evaluation of available statistics and the use of other input-output tables (derivative method). As it is possible to fill a given cell of the matrix by calculating both the input of the sector (column) and the output (row), a maximum of six figures could theoretically be derived for each cell. In reality, only one figure is calculated for each cell, depending on the most suitable method.

The major advantage of the input-output calculation is precisely the discipline that the rigid system of the table imposes on data collection and reciprocal control. In the Arequipa table column and row totals for some sectors (agriculture, industry, and trade) could be calculated through evaluation and projection of official statistics. The interaction figures (cells of the matrix) were first obtained directly, and then checked against other sources, where possible. In case of deviation, preference was given to directly obtained data rather than to the figures given in the statistics. The availability of some control totals from official data helped increase confidence in the reliability of the interaction figures. Due to the general lack of all data, no preference was given to any one data-collection method, and both input and output data were calculated. Nor was it possible to follow the procedure of concentrating only on the most important interrelationships, since not enough was known a priori concerning the extents of the interrelationships.

### Indirect Data Collection

The Arequipa table was filled in from the "outside to the inside"--i.e., the frame (total) data for the individual sectors were first calculated, and the cells were filled in later. For industry and mining the frame data, and especially the gross output value, could be obtained from the official statistics. Similar figures were also available for agriculture and trade, but they referred to previous years, so projections had to be made. Within the tertiary activities there were no compiled statistics but only data in individual subsectors, such as railways, banks, and so on. For other subsectors, such as road traffic, hotels, and so on, no useful figures were available at all; all data had to be obtained directly.

In the industry and trade sectors it was possible to obtain not only the data for the gross total output of the individual sectors from the official statistics but also interaction data. These were input figures that were, however, not broken down by regions, so they had to be supplemented by directly obtained data. Apart from this, a great deal of material, such as financial reports, budgets, and so on, was examined to obtain the input structure of the individual subsectors. These data then had to be assigned to regions through direct interviews.

In the derivative method existing input-output tables are taken as a basis, and the coefficients are used in other tables covering other regions or periods. In the Arequipa case two earlier input-output tables were available for reference: an input-output table for Peru from 1963 and, more important, an input-output table for Southern Peru, also from 1963.[2] The Peru table could not be used because in developing countries the structure of individual sectors varies so much in the different regions that an application of national coefficients to a regional table would lead to completely distorted results. The Southern Peru table is a regional table, and regions I and II of the Arequipa table are identical with the region it covers. Therefore, the Southern Peru table could be applied as a control in sectors that had not undergone any major structural changes between 1963 and 1968.

### Direct Data Collection

The direct interviews required to fill in an input-output table generally cover enterprises, public institutions, and households so that the figures for individual sectors can be obtained by aggregating their inputs and outputs. This technique was also applied in the present study. The first problems to be solved were the selection of the enterprises to be interviewed (samples) and the structure of the questionnaire.

In the agricultural sector a coverage of farms by interviews was not possible due to the short period of the field mission in Peru. Therefore, an attempt was made to obtain at least the interactions data through a transportation survey. The preconditions for this are very favorable in Arequipa, because road traffic to and from Arequipa is confined to two roads on which there are checkpoints where the police control the trucks and keep a record of all movements of goods. However, the evaluation of the police registers, which appeared to be so promising at the beginning, produced little useful data. The most important sources continued to be indirect calculations and direct interviews through sampling.

To obtain a satisfactory representation in sampling the basic unit should be as homogeneous as possible. To this end the sectors in the table were divided into the largest possible number of subsectors for the purposes of data collection; e.g., the wholesale-trade sector was divided into eight subsectors. In the industrial sectors the subsectors were generally identical with larger industrial firms, so in those cases where the questionnaires were answered total surveys were obtained.  In other cases the selection of samples only implied the coverage of a remainder of small enterprises.  As all enterprises were listed in the "Market Guide for Peru" by Dun and Bradstreet, only simple random sampling was necessary.

In the trade sectors some subsectors had a rather large number of firms.  In this case, average enterprises were selected according to the number of persons employed, or, if more than 50 percent of the total number of employed persons could be covered by selecting a few enterprises, these firms plus one or two of the smaller ones were interviewed.

In principle, the selection of the samples was not systematic but pragmatic; i.e., an attempt was made to cover the highest possible proportion of the total gross output value of the sector.  However, a certain bias toward larger enterprises cannot be denied.

Three questionnaires were prepared: one for industry and mining, one for trade, and one for transportation.  In the remaining sectors the interviews did not follow any fixed pattern.  The questionnaires were modelled on the questionnaires developed for the Philadelphia project,[3] and a questionnaire by Tiebout[4] for an input-output survey in California.

The questionnaires were first tested with some officials from ORDESUR in several enterprises and modified where necessary. Despite this, there were still some difficulties of comprehension in some items of the final questionnaire, and several questions proved to be unnecessary.  The interviews generally began with a brief introductory talk after which the questionnaire was left with the firms. It was seldom possible to get immediate response from the owner or the manager.  When the questionnaire was collected there was another discussion on items that were not clear or on interesting problems of the sector or subsector concerned.

The attitude of the respondents varied a great deal.  A number of firms said very pointedly that they had already had a large number of questionnaires from different ministries or that the interview interfered with the preparation of the annual accounts due at the end of the year.  Overwork was generally the most important reason given by those who declined to answer the questionnaire (about 20 percent).

The data appeared to be very reliable when based on figures supplied by records of enterprises.  The figures on the regional distribution of inputs and outputs had to be estimated by the respondents and were therefore less accurate.  But the estimates of the manager of a firm are still much more accurate than those of an outsider, however much the latter may know about the sector concerned.

There were no truly reliable means of ascertaining or controlling the amount of false information given, although rough checks could be made by comparison with data obtained from other sources. There was some reluctance to answer questions on taxes. No attempt was made to get direct responses on profits; these were estimated indirectly from other figures.

The compilation of data for the final table was based on the preliminary tables that were constructed for the individual sectors. The input and output totals were entered in the main table by the individual investigators. As an attempt has been made to cover as much input and output data as possible, two figures appeared in many cells of the final table, the input figure to the left and the output figure to the right. After entering all the available data, each investigator had to revise his sector.

At the end of this coordination phase substantial figures under "Undistributed" were to be found only in the local government and household sectors. There was no purpose in distributing the undistributed amounts under government and households, as the former was insufficiently covered and the households data were treated as a residual.

## SOME APPLICATIONS OF THE AREQUIPA TABLE

One important result of the Peru case study was the realization that it is possible to construct an interregional table for a developing region on the basis of direct and indirect data collection. In particular, the tertiary activities, which generally do not play a prominent role in input–output tables and which have an inadequate basis, can be included in an input–output table. The conceptual problems that arose in this field--e.g., the accounting in the trade and the public sector and the treatment of supraregional institutions--could be solved to a certain extent, even if the solutions were not wholly satisfactory.

The time and effort required to construct the Arequipa table were considerable. It required two sets of surveys, each lasting for three months, the first time with seven and the second time with three team members. Including the preparatory and the postsurvey evaluation period, this amounts to about 70 man-months for the entire study. If one takes into account the fact that the effort is naturally greater for a "pilot" study than for a routine job, one may assume 40 man-months to be a realistic estimate of the time requirements for the initial construction of an input–output table. If two years are calculated for the construction of such a table, then a regional planning authority must have at least two experts (plus auxiliary staff) at its disposal. On the other hand, as most of the essential data needed for regional planning as a whole can be obtained through an inter-regional input-output table, the effort would seem to be quite worth-while and probably a least-cost procedure.

The main question that arose in regional planning in Southern Peru concerned the extent to which the expansion of the growth pole of Arequipa would promote the development of the Southern Region.

Arequipa's spread effects are shown in the input-output table in the third quadrant, Arequipa's imports from the hinterland (see Table 7.1). The most important items here are agricultural raw materials for the households, chiefly meat (233 million soles, or $5.1 million); agricultural raw materials for industry, chiefly milk and wool (161 million soles, or $3.6 million); and semimanufactured products for industry, chiefly wool yarn, brewery, malt, and so on (72 million soles, or $1.6 million). These commonly tend to be the most important spread-effect sectors.

The input-output table permits an investigation of the effects that the growth of Arequipa, either in the form of a general income increase or in the form of the expansion of certain sectors, will have on the hinterland.

An investigation of the input structure of the households of Arequipa shows that only 10 percent of the inputs originate from the hinterland (see Table 7.2). Of the 257 million soles, or $5.8 mil-lion (see Table 7.1), 168 million soles, or $3.5 million, are for meat from the Andes regions. Most of the other agricultural prod-ucts are either produced in the oasis of Arequipa or imported.* The reason for this is the confinement of agriculture to irrigated areas in the dry desert zones and the fact that the climate in Andes regions permits only the supply of meat. The great tropical forest east of the Andes has not yet been opened up. The growth of Arequipa will, therefore, have very negligible spread effects and will only lead to an increase of imports, unless new irrigation projects are initiated in the coastal zone or the tropical forest area is opened up and col-onized. The Majes irrigation project close to Arequipa that the gov-ernment has initiated will create the prerequisites for stronger spread effects, particularly in the household and food-industry (milk) sectors. There are also long-term plans to open up a

--------

*The imports of the households are not indicated directly in the table, as an interview of households could not be carried out. A part of the imports are shown in Table 7.3, row 37; a large part (e.g., flour, bread) is entered in the fourth sector, "Food industry" (mills and bakeries).

TABLE 7.1

Aggregated Input-Output Table, Arequipa, Southern Peru, 1968
(millions of soles)*

| | Agriculture | Industry | Trade | Services | Households | Σ 1-5 | Agriculture | Mining | Industry | Trade | Services | Households | Σ 6-11 | Σ 1-11 | Exports | Other | TPV |
|---|---|---|---|---|---|---|---|---|---|---|---|---|---|---|---|---|---|
| 1. Agriculture | 122 | 33 | | 1 | 238 | 394 | 43 | 6 | 63 | | 6 | 5 | 5 | 399 | 169 | 57 | 625 |
| 2. Industry | 20 | 327 | 5 | 46 | 752 | 1,150 | 5 | 9 | 18 | 29 | 4 | 357 | 475 | 1,625 | 1,294 | 250 | 3,169 |
| 3. Trade | 4 | 32 | | 41 | 473 | 550 | | | 28 | | 11 | 199 | 235 | 785 | 64 | 32 | 881 |
| 4. Services | 27 | 178 | 119 | 49 | 697 | 1,070 | 44 | 10 | 12 | | 21 | 233 | 355 | 1,425 | 144 | 100 | 1,669 |
| 5. Households | 287 | 476 | 482 | 1,022 | | 2,267 | | 72 | | | 27 | | 84 | 2,351 | | 325 | 2,676 |
| Σ 1-5 Arequipa | 460 | 1,046 | 606 | 1,159 | 2,160 | 5,431 | 92 | 97 | 121 | 29 | 21 | 794 | 1,154 | 6,585 | 1,671 | 764 | 9,020 |
| 6. Agriculture | 44 | 161 | 4 | 1 | 233 | 439 | 1,505 | | 339 | | 1 | 3,286 | 5,157 | 5,596 | 641 | 17 | 6,254 |
| 7. Mining | 2 | 1 | | 1 | 1 | 5 | | 5 | 21 | | 29 | 6 | 28 | 33 | 6,010 | | 6,043 |
| 8. Industry | 3 | 72 | | 1 | | 76 | 11 | 18 | 57 | | 45 | 483 | 585 | 661 | 596 | 323 | 1,580 |
| 9. Trade | | | | 2 | | 2 | 2 | | 33 | 108 | 101 | 804 | 902 | 904 | 32 | 18 | 954 |
| 10. Services | | 21 | | 4 | 23 | 52 | 135 | 234 | 150 | | 2,329 | 2,132 | 2,860 | 2,912 | 179 | 134 | 3,225 |
| 11. Households | | 11 | | 6 | | 17 | 4,509 | 469 | 260 | 544 | 27 | | 8,111 | 8,128 | | 1,728 | 9,856 |
| Σ 6-11 Hinterland | 49 | 266 | 4 | 15 | 257 | 591 | 6,162 | 726 | 860 | 652 | 2,532 | 6,711 | 17,643 | 18,234 | 7,458 | 2,220 | 27,912 |
| Σ 1-11 S. Peru | 509 | 1,312 | 610 | 1,174 | 2,417 | 6,022 | 6,254 | 823 | 981 | 681 | 2,553 | 7,505 | 18,797 | 24,819 | 9,129 | 2,984 | 36,932 |
| 12. Imports | 47 | 1,087 | 27 | 213 | | 1,374 | | 1,107 | 279 | 29 | 305 | | 1,720 | 3,094 | | | |
| 13. Other | 69 | 770 | 244 | 282 | 259 | 1,624 | | 4,113 | 320 | 244 | 367 | 2,351 | 7,395 | 9,019 | | | |
| 14. TPV | 625 | 3,169 | 881 | 1,669 | 2,676 | 9,020 | 6,254 | 6,043 | 1,580 | 954 | 3,225 | 9,856 | 27,912 | 36,932 | | | |

Note: TPV = total production value.

*44 soles = $1.

TABLE 7.2

Matrix of Coefficients of the Aggregated Input-Output Table for Arequipa

| | Arequipa | | | | | Hinterland | | | | | |
|---|---|---|---|---|---|---|---|---|---|---|---|
| | Agriculture | Industry | Trade | Services | Households | Agriculture | Mining | Industry | Trade | Services | Households |
| **Arequipa** | | | | | | | | | | | |
| 1. Agriculture | 0.20 | 0.01 | | | 0.09 | 0.01 | | 0.04 | | | 0.04 |
| 2. Industry | 0.03 | 0.10 | 0.01 | 0.03 | 0.28 | | | 0.01 | | | 0.02 |
| 3. Trade | 0.01 | 0.01 | | 0.03 | 0.18 | | | | | | 0.02 |
| 4. Services | 0.04 | 0.06 | 0.14 | 0.03 | 0.26 | | | 0.02 | 0.03 | | |
| 5. Households | 0.46 | 0.15 | 0.55 | 0.61 | | 0.01 | 0.01 | 0.01 | | | |
| **Hinterland** | | | | | | | | | | | |
| 6. Agriculture | 0.07 | 0.05 | | | 0.09 | 0.24 | | 0.21 | | 0.01 | 0.33 |
| 7. Mining | | | | | | | | 0.01 | | | |
| 8. Industry | | 0.02 | | | | | | 0.04 | | 0.01 | 0.05 |
| 9. Trade | | | | | | | | 0.02 | | 0.01 | 0.08 |
| 10. Services | | 0.01 | | | 0.01 | 0.02 | 0.04 | 0.09 | 0.11 | 0.03 | 0.22 |
| 11. Households | | | | | | 0.72 | 0.08 | 0.16 | 0.57 | 0.72 | |
| 12. Imports | 0.08 | 0.34 | 0.03 | 0.13 | | | 0.18 | 0.18 | 0.03 | 0.09 | |
| 13. Others | 0.11 | 0.25 | 0.27 | 0.17 | 0.09 | | 0.69 | 0.21 | 0.26 | 0.13 | 0.24 |
| 14. Gross Total Outlay | 1.00 | 1.00 | 1.00 | 1.00 | 1.00 | 1.00 | 1.00 | 1.00 | 1.00 | 1.00 | 1.00 |

TABLE 7.3

Input–Output Table, Arequipa and Hinterland, Southern Peru, 1968
(millions of soles)*

| Outputs / Inputs | Arequipa | | | | | | | | | | | | | | | |
|---|---|---|---|---|---|---|---|---|---|---|---|---|---|---|---|---|
| | 1. | 2. | 3. | 4. | 5. | 6. | 7. | 8. | 9. | 10. | 11. | 12. | 13. | 14. | 15. | Σ 1-15 |
| **Arequipa** | | | | | | | | | | | | | | | | |
| 1. Livestock | 11 | 12 | | 32 | | | | | | | | | 1 | | 93 | 149 |
| 2. Agriculture | 57 | 42 | | 1 | | | | | | | | | | | 145 | 245 |
| 3. Mining | | | | | | | | 25 | 6 | | | | | | | 33 |
| 4. Food industry | 18 | | | 58 | | | | | | | | 1 | 4 | 2 | 365 | 448 |
| 5. Beverages industry | | | | | | | | | | | | | 3 | | 215 | 218 |
| 6. Textile industry | | | | 1 | | 13 | | | 1 | | | | 2 | 3 | 65 | 85 |
| 7. Metalworking industry | | | | 123 | | | 10 | | 8 | | | 19 | 1 | 3 | 36 | 200 |
| 8. Other industries | | 2 | | 11 | 4 | 14 | 4 | 13 | 36 | 4 | 1 | | 2 | 6 | 69 | 166 |
| 9. Building and construction | | | | | | | | | | | | | | | | |
| 10. Wholesale trade | | 4 | 2 | 12 | 1 | 5 | | 1 | 5 | | | 9 | 7 | 7 | 197 | 250 |
| 11. Retail trade | | | | | | | | | 6 | | | 6 | 6 | 6 | 276 | 300 |
| 12. Transport | 1 | 14 | | 24 | 10 | 8 | 16 | 14 | 17 | 43 | 28 | 3 | 6 | 5 | 220 | 409 |
| 13. Services | 7 | 4 | 2 | 30 | 9 | 18 | 7 | 20 | 3 | 37 | 11 | 15 | 15 | 5 | 163 | 346 |
| 14. Government (local) | 1 | | | | | | | | | | | | | | 314 | 315 |
| 15. Households | 27 | 260 | 12 | 153 | 57 | 71 | 29 | 93 | 61 | 285 | 197 | 329 | 284 | 409 | | 2,267 |
| Σ 1-15 | 122 | 338 | 16 | 445 | 81 | 129 | 66 | 166 | 143 | 369 | 237 | 382 | 331 | 446 | 2,160 | 5,431 |
| **Hinterland** | | | | | | | | | | | | | | | | |
| 16. Livestock | 38 | | | 115 | | 25 | | 13 | | | | | | | 210 | 401 |
| 17. Agriculture | | 6 | | 3 | 1 | | | 4 | | | | 1 | | | 23 | 38 |
| 18. Mining | | 2 | | 1 | | | | | | | | 1 | | | 1 | 5 |
| 19. Food industry | | | | 2 | 6 | | | | | | | | | | | 8 |
| 20. Beverages industry | | | | | 29 | | | | | | | | | | | 29 |
| 21. Textile industry | | | | | | 30 | | | | | | | | | | 30 |
| 22. Metalworking industry | | | | | | | | | | | | 1 | | | | 1 |
| 23. Other industries | | 3 | | | | | | 4 | 1 | | | | | | | 8 |
| 24. Building and construction | | | | | | | | | | | | | | | | |
| 25. Wholesale trade | | | | | | | | | | | | | | | | |
| 26. Retail trade | | | | | | | | | | | | 2 | | | | 2 |
| 27. Transport | | | | 4 | 7 | 2 | 3 | 3 | 1 | 3 | 1 | | | 1 | 6 | 31 |
| 28. Services | | | | | 1 | | | | | | | 3 | | | 6 | 10 |
| 29. Government (local) | | | | | | | | | | | | | | | 11 | 11 |
| 30. Households | | | | | 11 | | | | | | | 2 | 4 | | | 17 |
| Σ 16-30 | 38 | 11 | | 125 | 55 | 57 | 3 | 24 | 2 | 3 | 1 | 8 | 6 | 1 | 257 | 591 |
| Σ 1-30 | 160 | 349 | 16 | 570 | 136 | 186 | 69 | 190 | 145 | 372 | 238 | 390 | 337 | 447 | 2,417 | 6,022 |
| **Southern Peru** | | | | | | | | | | | | | | | | |
| 31. National imports | 2 | 8 | 12 | 98 | 52 | 68 | 119 | 75 | 17 | 13 | 14 | 109 | 29 | 28 | | 644 |
| 32. International imports | 1 | 36 | | 399 | 7 | 20 | 136 | 84 | | | | 27 | 5 | 15 | | 730 |
| 33. Central government | 2 | 13 | 3 | 88 | 89 | 26 | 12 | 12 | 4 | 125 | 102 | 77 | 29 | 16 | | 598 |
| 34. Factor payments | | | | 193 | 52 | 44 | 18 | 12 | | | | 6 | 15 | | | 340 |
| 35. Depreciation | 1 | 8 | 2 | 15 | 14 | 22 | 13 | 38 | 18 | 10 | 7 | 111 | 23 | | | 282 |
| 36. Undistributed | 45 | | | 55 | | | | 40 | | | | | | 5 | 259 | 404 |
| 37. Total inputs | 211 | 414 | 33 | 1,418 | 350 | 366 | 367 | 451 | 184 | 520 | 361 | 720 | 438 | 511 | 2,676 | 9,020 |

*44 soles = $1.

128

| 16. | 17. | 18. | 19. | 20. | 21. | 22. | 23. | 24. | 25. | 26. | 27. | 28. | 29. | 30. |
|---|---|---|---|---|---|---|---|---|---|---|---|---|---|---|
|  |  |  |  |  |  |  |  |  |  |  |  |  |  | 5 |
| 43 |  |  |  |  |  |  |  |  |  |  |  |  |  | 177 |
|  |  |  |  |  |  |  |  |  |  |  |  |  |  | 118 |
|  |  |  |  |  | 21 |  |  |  |  |  |  |  | 1 | 21 |
|  |  | 1 |  |  |  |  |  | 4 |  |  | 4 |  |  | 10 |
|  |  | 5 | 1 |  |  |  | 2 | 35 |  |  |  |  | 1 | 31 |
| 1 | 4 | 9 | 2 | 1 | 4 |  |  | 9 |  |  |  |  | 1 | 153 |
|  |  |  |  |  |  |  |  | 2 |  |  | 2 | 1 |  | 46 |
| 6 | 14 | 8 | 6 | 7 | 1 |  | 1 | 5 | 17 | 4 |  | 1 | 4 | 56 |
| 13 | 11 | 2 | 2 | 2 | 1 |  | 2 | 1 | 6 | 2 | 4 | 1 | 1 | 26 |
|  |  |  |  |  |  |  |  |  |  |  |  |  |  | 151 |
|  |  | 72 |  | 12 |  |  |  |  |  |  |  |  |  |  |
| 63 | 29 | 97 | 11 | 22 | 27 |  | 5 | 56 | 23 | 6 | 10 | 3 | 8 | 794 |
|  |  |  |  | 13 |  |  |  |  |  |  |  | 1 | 11 | 1,056 |
| 1,117 | 388 |  | 272 | 17 | 33 |  | 3 | 1 |  |  |  | 1 | 14 | 2,230 |
|  |  |  | 1 |  |  |  | 12 | 8 |  |  |  | 1 |  | 6 |
|  |  |  | 5 | 5 |  |  |  |  |  |  |  | 4 | 3 | 122 |
|  |  |  |  |  |  |  |  |  |  |  |  | 2 |  | 240 |
|  |  |  |  |  |  |  |  | 1 |  |  |  | 2 | 6 | 90 |
|  | 2 |  |  |  |  |  |  | 3 |  |  | 5 | 2 | 5 | 18 |
|  | 9 | 5 |  |  |  |  |  | 43 |  |  |  |  |  | 13 |
|  | 2 | 18 | 13 | 2 | 2 |  | 1 | 11 |  |  |  | 10 | 9 | 379 |
|  |  |  |  |  |  |  |  | 4 |  |  |  | 15 | 11 | 425 |
| 17 | 40 | 36 | 13 | 10 | 3 | 1 | 2 | 12 | 37 | 10 | 1 | 19 | 4 | 185 |
| 37 | 41 | 198 | 32 | 28 | 14 | 9 | 22 | 4 | 44 | 17 | 18 | 30 | 7 | 370 |
|  |  |  |  |  |  |  |  |  |  |  |  |  | 22 | 1,577 |
| 563 | 3,946 | 469 | 57 | 61 | 19 | 7 | 25 | 91 | 259 | 285 | 355 | 581 | 1,393 |  |
| 1,734 | 4,428 | 726 | 393 | 123 | 84 | 17 | 65 | 178 | 340 | 312 | 379 | 668 | 1,485 | 6,711 |
| 1,797 | 4,457 | 823 | 404 | 145 | 111 | 17 | 70 | 234 | 363 | 318 | 389 | 671 | 1,493 | 7,505 |
|  |  | 386 | 67 | 46 |  | 13 | 26 | 25 | 10 | 19 | 80 | 109 | 46 |  |
|  |  | 721 | 88 | 4 |  | 6 | 4 |  |  |  | 25 | 21 | 24 |  |
|  |  | 1,453 | 4 | 63 |  |  |  | 14 | 103 | 122 | 41 | 82 | 47 |  |
|  |  | 2,103 |  | 7 |  |  |  |  |  |  | 13 |  |  |  |
|  |  | 557 |  | 12 |  |  | 6 | 30 | 10 | 9 | 110 | 74 |  |  |
|  |  |  | 166 |  | 18 |  |  |  |  |  |  |  |  | 2,351 |
| 1,797 | 4,457 | 6,043 | 729 | 277 | 129 | 36 | 106 | 303 | 486 | 468 | 658 | 957 | 1,610 | 9,856 |

(continued)

TABLE 7.3 (continued)

| Outputs | | | Southern Peru | | | | | |
|---|---|---|---|---|---|---|---|---|
| | | | Nat'l Exp. | Int'l Exp. | Central Govt. | Investments | Undistributed | Gross Total Output |
| Inputs | Σ 16-30 | Σ 1-30 | 32. | 33. | 34. | 36. | 37. | 38. |
| Arequipa | | | | | | | | |
| 1. Livestock | | 149 | 62 | | | | | 211 |
| 2. Agriculture | 5 | 250 | 88 | 19 | | | 57 | 414 |
| 3. Mining | | 33 | | | | | | 33 |
| 4. Food industry | 220 | 668 | 715 | 9 | | | 26 | 1,418 |
| 5. Beverages industry | 118 | 336 | 14 | | | | | 350 |
| 6. Textile industry | 43 | 128 | 230 | 1 | | 7 | | 366 |
| 7. Metalworking industry | 19 | 219 | 128 | | 1 | 19 | | 367 |
| 8. Other industries | 75 | 241 | 182 | 15 | | 5 | 8 | 451 |
| 9. Building and construction | | | | | | 184 | | 184 |
| 10. Wholesale trade | 184 | 434 | 11 | 53 | | 12 | 10 | 520 |
| 11. Retail trade | 51 | 351 | | | | 10 | | 361 |
| 12. Transport | 130 | 539 | 81 | 8 | 43 | | 49 | 720 |
| 13. Services | 74 | 420 | 14 | 4 | | | | 438 |
| 14. Government (local) | 151 | 466 | 37 | | | | 8 | 511 |
| 15. Households | 84 | 2,351 | | | 325 | | | 2,676 |
| Σ 1-15 | 1,154 | 6,585 | 1,562 | 109 | 369 | 237 | 158 | 9,020 |
| Hinterland | | | | | | | | |
| 16. Livestock | 1,081 | 1,482 | 96 | 211 | | | 8 | 1,797 |
| 17. Agriculture | 4,076 | 4,114 | 182 | 152 | | | 9 | 4,457 |
| 18. Mining | 28 | 33 | 29 | 5,981 | | | | 6,043 |
| 19. Food industry | 139 | 147 | 63 | 519 | | | | 729 |
| 20. Beverages industry | 242 | 271 | 3 | | | | 3 | 277 |
| 21. Textile industry | 99 | 129 | | | | | | 129 |
| 22. Metalworking industry | 35 | 36 | | | | | | 36 |
| 23. Other industries | 70 | 78 | 11 | | | | 17 | 106 |
| 24. Building and construction | | | | | | 303 | | 303 |
| 25. Wholesale trade | 447 | 447 | | 32 | | 7 | | 486 |
| 26. Retail trade | 455 | 457 | | | | 11 | | 468 |
| 27. Transport | 390 | 421 | 84 | 44 | 59 | | 50 | 658 |
| 28. Services | 871 | 881 | 23 | 28 | | | 25 | 957 |
| 29. Government (local) | 1,599 | 1,610 | | | | | | 1,610 |
| 30. Households | 8,111 | 8,128 | | | 1,728 | | | 9,856 |
| Σ 16-30 | 17,643 | 18,234 | 491 | 6,967 | 1,787 | 321 | 112 | 27,912 |
| Σ 1-30 | 18,797 | 24,819 | 2,053 | 7,076 | 2,156 | 558 | 270 | 36,932 |
| Southern Peru | | | | | | | | |
| 31. National imports | 827 | 1,471 | | | | | | |
| 32. International imports | 893 | 1,623 | | | | | | |
| 33. Central government | 1,929 | 2,527 | | | | | | |
| 34. Factor payments | 2,123 | 2,463 | | | | | | |
| 35. Depreciation | 808 | 1,090 | | | | | | |
| 36. Undistributed | 2,535 | 2,939 | | | | | | |
| 37. Total inputs | 27,912 | 36,932 | | | | | | |

130

colonization area in the tropical forest zone. The construction of a new road from Arequipa to Juliaca has already been commenced; a feeder road leading from the Juliaca area to the northern departamento of Puno in the direction of Puerto Maldonado appears to be absolutely essential.

The share of inputs from the hinterland is even lower in industry than it is in households. Of the inputs 34 percent are imported (see Table 7.2), but only 5 percent of all inputs are agricultural products, and 2 percent are semimanufactured products from the hinterland. Therefore, the general expansion of the industry of Arequipa will only have slight effects on the hinterland. However, the situation varies greatly in the different sectors and subsectors. As the analysis of the 38 x 38 table shows (see Table 7.3), the hinterland supplies 16 percent of the inputs in the beverages industry (above all, malt for the breweries); in the textile industry this figure amounts to 15 percent (cotton and wool); in the food industry, to 9 percent (chiefly milk for the condensed milk plant). In the subsector "Milk processing" the input from the hinterland even goes as high as 22 percent. An increase in the production of condensed milk would therefore have a strong spread effect on the hinterland. The problem, however, lies in the limited supplies from the hinterland. This means that spread effects can only be achieved by implementing the Majes irrigation project mentioned above.

Unfortunately, most industrial sectors with a relatively high proportion of inputs from the hinterland have only low growth potentials, and so no spread effects can be expected. On the other hand, the industrial sectors with good growth chances (metalworking and electrical appliances) have hardly any transactions with the hinterland and will hardly be able to develop them in the foreseeable future. Spread effects in this field can only be achieved via subcontracting industries in Arequipa and via income--i.e., through the households sector.

To sum up, the Arequipa case study has clearly revealed that a vague concept to develop stagnating areas through the spread effects of growth poles has little value in practice. The regional planner should apply an interregional input-output table to determine the sectors that have meaningful interrelationships with the hinterland and then identify complementary investments in the hinterland in order to make the achievement of technically feasible spread effects a reality.

NOTES

1.  P. P. Waller (ed.), <u>La Cuantificacion de las Relaciones</u> <u>Ciudad Area de Influencia mediante el Metodo de Insumo Producto</u>, vol. 1, Parte General (Informe Provisional) (Berlin:  GDI, 1970); vol. 2, Documentacion de los Sectores (Berlin: GDI, 1972).

2.  D. F. Schreiner and J. F. Timmons, <u>An Integrated</u> <u>Growth Model for the Basic Sectors of Southern Peru</u> (Ames, Iowa: State University, Department of Economics, 1968).

3.  W. Isard, T. W. Langford, and E. Romanoff, <u>Philadelphia</u> <u>Region Input–Output Study</u> (Philadelphia:  Regional Science Research Institute, 1967).

4.  C. Tiebout, <u>The Community Economic Base Study</u> (New York:  Committee for Economic Development, 1962).

AVROM BENDAVID-VAL resides in the Washington, D.C. area, where he engages in private practice through his firm, Joint Venture 2, specializing in development, public interest, and social economics. He has been a teacher, analyst, and planner in regional development in Israel, Thailand, Holland, and the United States. He has published articles in the International Development Review, International Journal of Social Economics, and elsewhere and is author of Regional Economic Analysis for Practitioners (New York: Praeger, 1974). Mr. Bendavid-Val holds an M.A. degree in regional and development economics from the University of Maryland.

PETER P. WALLER is head of the Africa Section at the German Development Institute in West Berlin. He is engaged in postgraduate teaching and consulting for the German government, primarily in the field of regional planning. He has conducted field projects in Afghanistan, Peru, Kenya, Zambia, Madagascar, and elsewhere. Dr. Waller received his M.A. in economics and his Ph.D. in economic geography from the University of Munich and worked at the University of British Columbia as a lecturer in geography. He is coauthor of Periodic Markets, Urbanization and Regional Planning: A Case Study from Western Kenya (Westport: Greenwood Press, 1976) and has published various articles in Economic Geography, East-African Geographical Journal, Geographische Rundschau, and Die Erde, among others.

DIETER WEISS is head of the Middle-East Section at the German Development Institute. His field experience was gathered principally in Tunisia, Egypt, India, Pakistan, and Nepal. He is author of Planning Social Overhead Investments (Berlin: Hessling, 1971, in German). He has a Dipl. Ing., and a Dr. rer. pol.

CHRISTIAN HEIMPEL is head of the Europe Section at the German Development Institute. His major field projects have been in Brazil, Mozambique, Ethiopia, India, and Taiwan. He is author of Approaches to Planning Agricultural Development Projects (Berlin: Hessling, 1973, in German). He has a Dipl. Landwirt and a Dr. rer. pol.

MARTIN SCHÜMER is a staff member of the German Development Institute. He has field experience in Brazil, Kenya, Zambia, and Malawi. He has a Dipl. Politologe from the Free University of Berlin.

THE AGRICULTURAL DEVELOPMENT OF TURKEY
Oddvar Aresvik

DEVELOPMENT IN RICH AND POOR COUNTRIES:
A General Theory with Statistical Analyses
Thorkil Kristensen

MERCHANTS AS PROMOTERS OF RURAL
DEVELOPMENT: An Indian Case Study
Paul A. London

NEW DIRECTIONS IN DEVELOPMENT: Latin
America, Export Credit, Population Growth, and
U.S. Attitudes. (Overseas Development Council
Studies--II)
Colin I. Bradford, Jr.,
Nathaniel McKitterick,
B. Jenkins Middleton,
William Rich,
Paul A. Laudicina

*PATTERNS OF POVERTY IN THE THIRD WORLD:
A Study of Social and Economic Stratification
Charles Elliott, assisted
by Françoise de Morsier

*REGIONAL ECONOMIC ANALYSIS FOR
PRACTITIONERS: An Introduction to Common
Descriptive Methods
revised edition
Avrom Bendavid

*THE U.S. AND WORLD DEVELOPMENT:
AGENDA FOR ACTION, 1975
James W. Howe and the
Staff of the Overseas
Development Council

*Also available in paperback as a Praeger Special Studies
Student Edition.